FUSING FUN!
Fast Fearless Art Quilts

LAURA WASILOWSKI

Text © 2005 Laura Wasilowski

Artwork © 2005 C&T Publishing, Inc.

Publisher: Amy Marson

Editorial Director: Gailen Runge

Acquisitions Editor: Jan Grigsby

Editor: Lynn Koolish

Technical Editors: Catherine Comyns, Pat Wilens

Copyeditor/Proofreader: Wordfirm, Inc.

Cover Designer: Kristy A. Konitzer

Design Director/Book Designer: Kristy A. Konitzer

Illustrator: Matt Allen

Production Assistant: Matt Allen

Photography: Luke Mulks, except as noted

Published by C&T Publishing, Inc., P.O. Box 1456, Lafayette, California 94549

Front cover: *Tea Time* by Laura Wasilowski

Back cover: *Confetti Collage* by Laura Wasilowski

Library of Congress Cataloging-in-Publication Data

Wasilowski, Laura

  Fusing fun! : fast fearless art quilts / Laura Wasilowski.

    p. cm.

  Includes bibliographical references and index.

  ISBN 1-57120-289-7 (paper trade)

  1. Quilting--Patterns. 2. Patchwork--Patterns. I. Title.

  TT835.W374 2005

  746.46--dc22

                2004015850

Printed in China

10 9 8 7 6 5 4 3 2 1

CONTENTS

DEDICATION

To the people I love: Steve, Gus, and Louise

ACKNOWLEDGMENTS

I will always be grateful to my mother, Penelope, for my first treadle sewing machine and to my dad, Leo, for his inventive spirit. And thank you to my sweet husband, Steve, for his constant encouragement and sense of humor and to our lovely children, Gus and Louise, for enriching my life.

My gratitude goes to my entertaining father-in-law, Emil Wasilowski, for teaching me the basics of running a small business. And thanks go to my friend Denise Kavanaugh. She encouraged me to turn my art into a business and has provided a nurturing environment for so many artists at the Fine Line Creative Arts Center in St. Charles, Illinois.

Special thanks to my friend Janet Dye, who introduced me to quiltmaking. It was Janet who invited me to a lecture by Caryl Bryer Fallert, and it was Caryl who opened my eyes to the wonders of the art quilt.

My thanks to Melody Johnson, my song-writing partner, who introduced me to fusing. I am so lucky to know her and my other quilting friends, Frieda Anderson, Emily Parson, and fellow members of the Professional Art Quilters Alliance (PAQA).

I am very grateful to Lynn Koolish, Diane Pedersen, Catherine Comyns, Kristy Konitzer, and Jan Grigsby for their kind support.
I enjoyed working with them and all of the C&T staff.

And finally I would like to thank my students. They have taught me much more than I ever taught them.

I enjoyed writing this book. I wrote it on planes, trains, and automobiles, in a quiet basement studio, and at bustling quilt shows. My inspiration came from my students, fellow artists, and my own love of the art quilt.

Introduction
INTRODUCTION

To look at me you would think I was a mild-mannered quiltmaker, a sweet little old lady with granny glasses and a calico apron. But hidden behind this benign facade lurks a freewheeling fuser!

A fuser makes quilts with fusible web. My fused quilts won't keep you warm in winter. They don't decorate the guest-room bed. They are totally useless. Well, not totally useless. My quilts are meant to be viewed; they are pieces of art. When I make fused art quilts, I imagine myself as a quilting revolutionary, sort of a Rebel with a Stash.

I credit fusible web with making me the rebel that I am today. Fusible web is a glue that is transferred, or "fused," to fabric with the heat of an iron; the fused fabric can then be cut into any shape imaginable. Fusing is quick and easy.

PRESSING MATTERS, 41˝ × 51˝, by Laura Wasilowski
Photo by Laura Wasilowski

Why I Choose to Fuse

For me, fusing is the most direct route from a design idea to the implementation of that idea. I can proceed directly to the creation of quilts without stopping for technical roadblocks such as cutting templates, measuring seam allowances, piecing, or matching points. When those traditional construction methods are bypassed, the constraints on my creativity dissolve. My quiltmaking becomes less restricted, more inventive, loose, and free.

REBEL WITH A STASH: SELF-PORTRAIT #3, 17˝ × 23˝, by Laura Wasilowski

My method of creating fused art quilts is quite simple. I cut directly into fused fabric as if cutting a piece of paper. Scissors or rotary cutters become my drawing tools.

I seldom measure the fabrics I cut. It's very liberating to be free of measuring fabric; it's like estimating your weight rather than standing on the scale. I rely upon my eyes to set intuitive limits, and I trust my sense of play and improvisation to guide my hands. That way, the shapes I cut are uniquely my own.

In fusing, there are no sewn seams to limit the shapes I cut. The fabrics overlap each other, and the fusible web seals them together like glue on paper. I can easily cut, alter, move, layer, and reassemble the shapes.

From idea to end product, my creativity is focused on the design. When I fuse, I can work quickly. As a result, I produce more quilts. And the more quilts I make, the more I can explore and grow as an artist.

So why do I choose to fuse? I fuse because it's easy. It's fast, it's free, and it's fun! I fuse because fusing invites improvisation and grants endless possibilities.

So join the revolution and come fuse with me!

BLUE BOOK ON BLUE CHAIRS, 46″ × 47″, by Laura Wasilowski
Photo by Laura Wasilowski

A Guide to Fused Art Quilts

This book is your tour guide to the creation of fused art quilts. It's a map for new quiltmakers as well as seasoned professionals who want a change of venue. To make the trip worthwhile, become familiar with each chapter and discover what it has to offer. I hope you enjoy the scenery along the way.

Begin with **Getting Started** (pages 7–11), where you will learn about tools and materials for making fused quilts. In **Fusing Fundamentals** (pages 12–15), learn basic fusing skills and earn a Certificate of Fusology from the Chicago School of Fusing. This fictitious school is only a product of my imagination, but the skills you will learn are tangible and necessary to complete the projects successfully.

The seven quilt **projects** (pages 16–59) are presented in a progressive manner. Each quilt builds on the skills learned in preceding chapters. It will be to your advantage to work through the chapters, or at least preview them, in sequence. Each chapter also discusses design concepts such as balance, value, shape, and line and how they are applied to the quilt project.

Fused Finishing (pages 60–67) explains how to quilt and bind fused quilts. It also suggests display options for the pieces and care instructions for fused quilts. If you're feeling adventurous, read **Wild, Wild Web** (pages 68–70) for unusual applications of fusible web.

And finally, for even more inspiration, view the work in **An Inspirational Gallery of Fused Art Quilts** (pages 71–78). Works by talented artists at the height of their careers appear here. Each piece affirms the beauty and vibrancy of the fused art quilt.

Getting Started

GETTING STARTED

Like most quiltmakers, I can add, but I can't subtract. For example, I can easily add fabrics to my stash, but I have trouble subtracting or removing fabrics. Fortunately, fused quilts are made with traditional sewing tools and fabrics, so with the exception of fusible web, you don't need to add to the quiltmaking supplies you have at hand. But if you feel you must add fabric to your stash, go ahead; I understand.

Fusible Web

Fused quilts depend upon one basic tool, fusible web. Fusible web consists of a dry polyamide glue attached to a release (or backing) paper. When you feel the fusible web, the rough side is the glue and the smooth side is the release paper. This type of fusible web is often referred to as paper-backed fusible web.

The glue is activated by the heat of an iron and will transfer, or fuse, to fabric. After the fabric cools, the release paper is removed. The fabric can then be fused to another piece of fabric with an iron. You can find complete instructions on how to transfer fusible web to fabric on pages 12–13.

PRESSING THE ENVELOPE, 40˝ × 46˝, by Laura Wasilowski
Photo by Laura Wasilowski

Fusible web

There are several brands of fusible web. The easiest to use and most commonly available brands are regular-weight Wonder-Under Transfer Web by Pellon and Trans-Web by HTC. Bondaweb by Vilene is available in Great Britain. Other brands are available, but some are difficult to stitch through by hand or machine, and some fusible webs may gum up the needle. Test the web before purchasing it in large quantities.

In the United States, fusible web usually comes on 17˝-wide bolts. It is sold by the yard in the interfacing department of fabric and craft stores. Be sure to read the directions that come with the fusible web so your quilts will be properly fused.

Be kind to the fusible web. Roll it into a tube to keep it from creasing or wrinkling. Don't expose the web to the excess heat of a hot car or attic. Occasionally the web will separate from the paper even before it's transferred. The web is still usable, and you can fuse it by placing the release paper on top of the web and ironing it to the fabric.

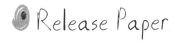

Release Paper

Fusible web comes with a protective sheet of paper called release paper. Release paper backs the web and holds it in place while you iron the glue to the fabric. It also protects the iron from the glue. After you iron the fusible web to the fabric, the release paper becomes "glueless." **Save this paper. It is invaluable.**

Release paper is a fuser's best friend. It's treated with a special lubricant so fused fabric can always be easily removed from it. For example, in a fused collage, fused fabrics are overlapped and fused into place on release paper. The collage can be removed, cut apart, reassembled, and re-fused to either side of the release paper any number of times.

Use release paper to store your fused fabric. Just roll up the fabric in the paper to keep the fabric from sticking to itself. Release paper is perfect for tracing patterns and transferring patterns to fused fabrics. (Refer to the Tea Time project on pages 27–33.) Release paper can also act as a pressing cloth to protect quilt tops, irons, and ironing surfaces from the web.

Throughout this book the term "release paper" refers to the backing paper after the fusible glue has been removed.

Fabric Selection

Choose your fabrics carefully. Almost any fabric that can withstand the high heat of an iron can be fused. Heavy fabrics, such as wool and felt, may not allow the iron's heat to penetrate through to the fusible web and may thus prevent fusing. On fine, transparent fabrics, the glue may seep through and leave a stain.

Fabrics with a coating, such as a permanent press finish, may not fuse well to other fabrics. There is no way to remove these coatings, which interfere with the bonding process. Some fabrics are treated with a sizing or starch that must be washed out before fusing. Even

fabric softeners used in the rinse cycle may prevent the glue from binding to the fabric tightly.

Medium-weight cottons, such as those commonly used for quiltmaking, work the best for fusing. Choose fabrics with a tight weave. Loosely woven fabrics tend to fray around the edges despite the glue on the back.

Many types of fabric work well for fusing.

My favorite type of fabric for fused art quilts is hand-dyed cotton rather than printed textiles. Most printed fabrics are stamped, so the ink rests on the top of the fabric. The wrong side of the fabric is almost white. In my fused quilts the edges are left unfinished, and any fraying of the printed fabric would reveal the white backing color. The color of a hand-dyed fabric penetrates through to the back of the fabric. And a hand-dyed fabric has no coatings or starches to hinder fusing. Other fabrics that work well are batiks and woven prints and solids.

If you aren't sure of the fiber content, the finish, or the fusibility of a fabric, experiment with a small swatch of it before investing in yardage. Some finicky fabrics can be protected from a hot iron with a pressing cloth or a barrier of release paper. Refer to **Wild, Wild Web** (pages 68–70) to learn more about fusing unusual fibers such as cheesecloth, lamé, silk, and paper.

A fused fabric can be used today or a year from today. It never loses its fusibility. Save all your fused scraps or cut-away fabrics. They will come in handy for the *Confetti Collage* project (page 55–59).

 Batting

The fused quilts in this book are layered into a quilt sandwich in the same manner as traditional quilts. There is the top layer of the sandwich, a filler or batting layer, and a backing fabric. An art quilt needs to hang flat against the wall for display. An essential ingredient in the creation of flat art quilts is a good stiff batting.

Avoid lofty polyester batting; it will not iron flat. Battings made of mostly cotton or 100% cotton work best for fused quilts. My favorite is Hobbs Heirloom Premium Cotton Batting made of 80% cotton and 20% polyester fibers. Both sides of the Hobbs batting work well; the batting grips fused fabrics, irons flat, and is easy to hand or machine quilt.

Your fused quilt will not be laundered, so there is no need to preshrink a 100% cotton batting. But before using a batting, test it. Some cotton battings have a scrim or a stabilizing coating applied to one side. Fused fabrics applied to the scrim side of the batting may shrink the scrim and cause the surface of the quilt to ripple. The ripples cannot be steamed flat. If you're not sure which side is the scrim side, test the batting before use.

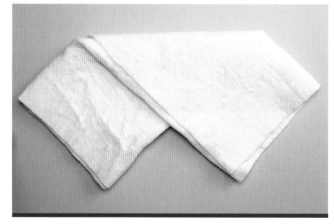

Low-loft cotton batting works best for fusing.

If you aren't sure whether your batting has a scrim, make a test sample by fusing fabric to both sides of the batting. If one side ripples, be sure to fuse your fabric to the side that doesn't ripple.

If you do mistakenly fuse your quilt to the scrim side of a batting, there is a tedious way to remove it. Heat the surface of the rippled quilt a section at a time with a hot iron and begin carefully peeling the quilt from the batting. Repeat until the entire top has been removed.

Manufacturers now produce pre-fused battings, battings with fusible web already applied to the surface. For the projects in this book, this type of batting is unnecessary because the fabrics applied to the batting already have fusible web on them.

Felt is another batting option. I use two layers of acrylic felt for small quilts and fuse directly to the felt. The felt holds the quilts flat and stiff. Always iron acrylic felt with a pressing cloth or protective sheet of release paper to keep the felt from singeing.

Thread

For fused quilts, the stitching or quilting not only is functional but often adds texture or embellishment to the quilt. Fusible web adds more body to fabric in a quilt. As a result, hand stitching through several layers of fused fabrics may be difficult. Embroidery threads in size 8, 12, or 14 are the easiest to stitch by hand. Use crewel or embroidery needles in sizes 3 to 9; select the size that works for the thread you are using. (Note: the *higher* the thread size or weight, the *thinner* the thread.)

Machine quilting through fused fabrics is easy. It's the same as machine quilting a nonfused quilt. With most machines, you can stitch through eight layers of fused fabric without difficulty. Most of my quilting is free-motion work with thread weights from 12 to 50. For more information on thread, refer to **Quilting the Fused Quilt** (pages 60–61).

Fused quilts can be quilted with many types of thread.

Scissors and Rotary Cutters

Many of the fabric edges in fused art quilts are not finished with stitching. This "raw edge" appliqué technique looks best when cut with sharp tools. A sharp pair of scissors yields crisp edges, whereas dull scissors fray fabric.

For fusing you will need three pairs of scissors. Use an inexpensive pair of paper scissors for cutting the fusible web. A standard-size pair of 8″ knife-edge fabric shears works for large lengths of fabric as well as large fused elements. For small elements, a pair of small, high-quality, sharp scissors is a good investment. I use 5″ knife-edge sewing scissors to cut tiny dots and squiggles.

Treat scissors kindly. Do not use fabric scissors to cut paper. Dropping scissors causes misalignment and burrs on the blades that hinder cutting. Having your scissors regularly honed by a reputable scissors sharpener is well worth the fee you pay.

Decorative blades for rotary cutters are remarkable cutting tools for fused fabrics. They come in shapes such as deckle, wave, scallop, or pinking. Although the blades may be labeled "for paper," they cut fused fabric cleanly. The blades fit into a standard-size rotary cutter. The embellished edge adds another level of line and texture to the fused quilt. To learn how to use decorative blades, refer to page 14.

Tweezers are handy tools for dealing with small fused shapes. They make it easy to pick up a shape and position it on the quilt.

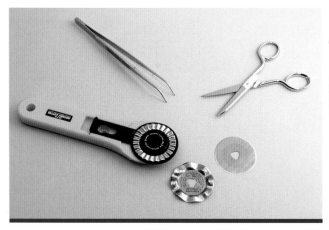

Scissors, tweezers, rotary cutter, and decorative blades

Irons and Ironing Surfaces

IRONS

A steam iron is a fuser's best friend. After you fuse a quilt with a dry iron, the fusible web must be set with a steam iron. You can use an iron with steam holes on the sole plate to dry fuse your fabric, and later you can use the same iron to steam set the piece. It's not the weight of the iron that creates the best bond between fused fabrics, but the heat. The iron does not have to be expensive, but it does need to reach and maintain a high heat (cotton setting) consistently.

A lightweight iron is important if you are doing a lot of fusing. Wand irons are especially handy when you are fusing many small elements. Wand irons need a holder or brace to keep them from falling over and scorching your quilt or the ironing surface. Placing a hot wand iron in a ceramic coffee mug also keeps it from falling or rolling over.

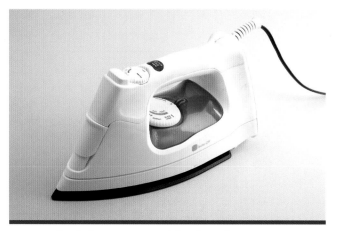

For fusing, use a good, hot iron that steams.

Many of the fabric edges are not stitched down, so it is especially important that the fabric is fused securely with steam.

Set up your ironing surface so that you won't trip over the cord or snag it on obstructions. There are products on the market to corral the iron and hold it out of the way. A dropped or damaged iron should be tested on scraps of fused fabric to make sure that it still holds its temperature and doesn't overheat and burn the fabric.

Keep your iron clean. Don't allow the fusible web to touch a hot iron, and don't iron the web onto the ironing surface. There are commercial iron-cleaning products on the market to remove the web from the iron. You can also try scraping off the glue by running the hot iron across a scrap fabric on the edge of your ironing board.

IRONING SURFACES

An ironing board generally works fine for fusing fabric. Ideally, you should have a large flat, padded ironing surface. The surface should be big enough to hold the entire length of fabric you are fusing and to allow you to cut the fusible web to size. A small, portable ironing pad (like for a workshop) works well if it is wide enough to accommodate at least the 17″ width of most fusible webs. For those of you who are committed to fusing, an ironing surface at waist height is much easier on the back.

Keep your ironing surface clean. Once the surface has fusible web stuck on it, the web may transfer to your iron, fabrics, or quilts. One option is to put down a piece of old fabric to protect the surface while fusing. If glue sticks to it, remove it and use a fresh piece of old fabric. A simpler option is to use a length of release paper on the ironing surface (make sure no fusible web is adhered to it). If web transfers to it, simply throw it away.

Protect your quilt top from glue that may have transferred to the iron. Place a piece of release paper (free of any fusible web) on the quilt when ironing. An additional benefit of using release paper is that a fused fabric mistakenly placed upside down will stick to it rather than to the iron.

Fusing Fundamentals
FUSING FUNDAMENTALS

There are several simple rules to follow when using fusible web. I call them Fusing Fundamentals 101. If you are familiar with these basic fusing procedures, you are guaranteed well-constructed quilts and many hours of fusing fun. After passing Fusing Fundamentals 101, my students receive the coveted Certificate in Fusology at the end of the class. You too can earn your certificate by following these easy guidelines.

DECIDUOUS DECORUM, 22″ × 20″, by Laura Wasilowski

◊ Fusing: Transferring Fusible Web to Fabric

1. Before you fuse fabric, wash it to remove sizing or fabric softener, which may interfere with the gluing process.

2. Place the fabric wrong side up on the ironing surface and iron it flat.

3. Read the directions that come with the fusible web regarding the heat setting for the iron. For cotton, use a hot dry iron on the cotton setting. The directions also recommend the length of time to leave the iron in place when ironing the web to the fabric. For example, the makers of Wonder-Under suggest leaving the iron in place for 5 seconds.

4. Examine the fusible web attached to the release paper and feel the texture. The glue side is bumpy and rough. The nonglue side is the smooth release paper that protects the hot iron from the glue.

5. Place the fusible web on top of the wrong side of the fabric. The rough side, or glue side, of the web touches the fabric. The release paper is on top.

6. Cut the fusible web to size. Cut it slightly smaller than the fabric by about $^1/_{16}$″ to $^1/_8$″. By cutting it smaller, you protect the ironing surface from the glue.

Cut the web smaller than the fabric.

7. Heat the iron to the proper setting. At this time, ***do not*** use the steam setting on the iron. You are just "tacking" the web to the fabric; the final fusing comes after the shapes are cut out and arranged on your quilt top.

8. Apply the iron to the release paper and hold in place for the prescribed time (about 5 seconds). Move the iron slowly across the fabric so every inch is covered for the recommended amount of time.

9. Do not over-fuse. If you apply the iron for too long in one spot, the fusible web will dissolve into the fabric and lose its strength.

10. Do not apply extra pressure to the iron. Let the heat and the weight of the iron do the work for you.

11. Occasionally, the release paper and fabric will appear to ripple when fused. This rippling will disappear once the release paper is removed.

Release Paper

1. Let the fabric cool before testing the bond of glue to fabric.

2. Lift a corner of the release paper and separate it from the fabric. If the glue has transferred, the fabric will be covered with a dull film, and the release paper will pull off easily.

3. If the glue stretches between the fabric and the release paper, the web must be reheated. Check the iron temperature and reapply the iron. Hold the iron in place for 5 seconds.

4. After the fabric cools, remove the release paper all in one sheet. Begin by lifting the paper at a corner and slowly peeling it back a few inches. Slip your hand between the release paper and the fabric. Slowly swipe your hand back and forth to remove the sheet all in one piece.

5. Keep the release paper in one piece if possible. You will use it often when working with fused fabrics.

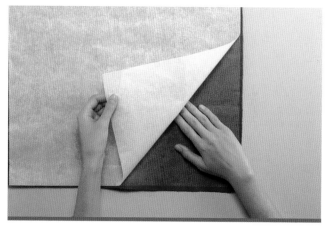

Remove the release paper in one sheet.

Cutting Fused Fabric

1. Always use sharp scissors and sharp rotary cutter blades when cutting fused fabrics. A clean, crisp cut looks best; dull scissors and rotary cutters fray fabric.

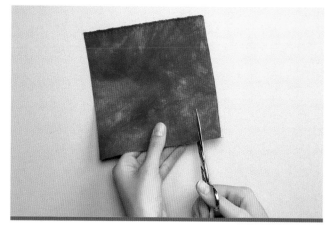

Use sharp scissors to cut fused fabrics.

2. Cutting through paper dulls scissors and rotary cutter blades, so remove the release paper before cutting the fabric.

3. If you do need to leave on the release paper to cut out a pattern piece, remove the release paper after cutting by gently scoring the paper in the center with the tip of the scissors. Pull off the paper outward from the center cut to keep the fabric from fraying around the edges.

4. When stacking two fused fabrics to cut out the same shape, do not place the fused sides together. They will stick together and be difficult to separate.

5. When cutting fabrics on a cutting mat, place fabrics fused side up. This way the glue won't stick to the mat, and the fabric won't fray when you remove it from the mat. Also, you can see whether you are cutting an area of the fabric where there is no fusible web.

Cutting with Decorative Blades

Decorative rotary cutter blades are available in scrapbooking stores and most craft stores. They may be labeled "for paper," but they work on fused fabrics as well. They come in shapes such as deckle, wave, pinking, and scallop.

1. Replace the straight blade on your standard-size rotary cutter with the decorative blade.

2. Remove the release paper from the fused fabric before cutting; the paper will dull the blades.

3. Cut the fabric on the back of the cutting mat to avoid nicking the grid lines.

4. Place the fabric fused side up so it doesn't stick to the mat.

5. Don't use a quilting ruler when you cut with decorative blades. The decorative blade may nick into the ruler and chip it. For a straight line, mark the fabric with chalk or just free-cut for organic shapes.

6. More pressure may be needed to cleanly cut with a decorative blade.

7. If the blade does not cut all the way through, use a small pair of scissors to finish the cut.

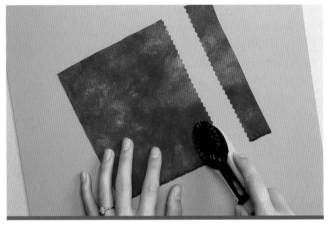

Use decorative rotary cutter blades to cut fused fabric.

Overlap/Under-lap Process

In fusing, there are no sewn seams. Fabrics are joined by overlapping or under-lapping them and fusing them together with an iron. An overlap or under-lap of about 1/4″ is sufficient to bond two fabrics together.

1. Whenever possible, overlap dark value fabrics on top of light value fabrics. Dark fabrics will show through light fabrics.

2. If a light value fabric piece must overlap a dark fabric, consider making two exact layers of the light value piece to conceal the dark fabric. Fuse one light-colored fabric to the top of another and then cut out the shape.

Overlap fused fabrics to seal them together.

Fuse–Tacking and Steam Setting

1. Fuse-tacking is lightly applying the iron for a minimum amount of time (about 5 seconds) to hold a fused fabric in place while constructing the quilt top. Applying too much heat to fusible web or applying the iron for too long will burn the glue into the fabric, and the fabric will no longer fuse to another fabric. **Remember, fuse-tack for only 5 seconds.**

2. To set the glue at the very end of construction, steam the quilt top for 10 seconds. Steam with a steam iron or damp cloth. This ensures a good bond between fabric and glue and flattens the quilt as well.

Iron and Quilt Protection

1. Keep the iron clean. Do not allow the fusible web to touch a hot iron at any time. The glue will melt to the iron and transfer to the quilt top or ironing surface. Glue is very difficult to remove from a quilt top, and it also picks up lint and dirt from the iron. (Refer to **Irons and Ironing Surfaces** on pages 10–11.)

2. Protect the quilt top from glue during construction by placing a pressing cloth or piece of release paper between the iron and quilt.

3. Do not allow the fusible web to transfer to the ironing surface. A hot iron may pick up the glue and transfer it to the quilt top. Protect the ironing surface with a pressing cloth or release paper.

4. If you fuse a fabric in the wrong position, you can remove it before steaming. Heat up the fabric piece with the iron and rip it off the surface. The fabric may fray and have to be replaced. Fibers and glue may remain on the quilt top. Scrape off frayed fabrics and glue with a fingernail, and fuse another piece of fabric on top.

5. Occasionally a fabric is placed fused side up and then trapped beneath other fused fabrics. Fuse another piece of fabric on top. It may change the design but it will cover the glue. Consider this a "design opportunity."

Congratulations! You have now received your Certificate in Fusology!

Posy Picture

A SIMPLE FREE-CUT FLOWER QUILT

POSY PICTURE, 8″ × 11″, by Laura Wasilowski

Everything I learned about cutting, I learned in kindergarten. My first art lesson: Cut out a fat circle from red construction paper and paste it to a blue background. It was so much fun!

Since that time, little has changed in my art making. I still rely upon that simple technique I learned called *free-cutting*. Free-cutting is cutting directly into fused fabric without using a pattern, diagram, template, or ruler. It's like cutting into construction paper without following any lines—like drawing with your scissors.

There's no wrong way to free-cut your fused fabrics. Soon you will develop your own free-cutting style, much like an individual signature or fingerprint. You may cut smooth curves or snip your way around a shape. No matter what your scissors style, free-cutting will set you free!

The *Posy Picture* is made by free-cutting the small pieces of the picture (flowers, leaves, and stems) from fused fabric. The pieces are arranged on a background fabric, fused into place, and embellished with hand embroidery stitches.

MATERIALS

Refer to pages 12–15 for complete descriptions of fusing techniques, including ironing fusible web to fabric, removing release paper, and fuse-tacking.

- **Flower fabric:** 6″ × 6″ of a medium value color
- **Flower center fabric:** 2″ × 4″ of a medium value color
- **Leaf fabric:** 6″ × 6″ of a medium value color
- **Stem fabric:** 2″ × 6″ of a medium value color
- **Background fabric:** 9″ × 12″ of a light value color

- **Binding fabric:** 6″ × 14″ of a medium value color
- **Backing fabric:** 9″ × 12″
- **Fusible web:** 1 yard
- **Batting:** 9″ × 12″
- **Size 8 or 12 hand embroidery thread** for quilting
- **Hand embroidery needle**

❀ Preparation

1. This quilt measures about 8″ × 11″ upon completion. It is hand quilted and embroidered and has a loop for hanging.

2. Assemble all the materials and tools listed.

3. Fuse all the fabrics—except the backing fabric—and remove the release paper.

❀ Posies

1. Use scissors to free-cut 3 squares about 2″ × 2″ from the flower fabric. You don't need to measure or draw the squares; just estimate the size and cut out pieces of fabric.

2. Trim the flower squares into circles.

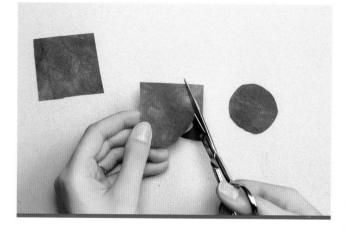

3. Snip out slivers of fabric around the circles to form the flower petals.

4. Free-cut a rectangle measuring about ³/₄″ by 4″ from the flower center fabric. To make a dot for the center of the flower, hold the end of the rectangle in one hand and place the scissors on the edge of the fabric. Slowly cut a circle. Rotate the fabric with one hand and hold the scissors steady as you move the fabric. Try to cut out the circle in one smooth cut.

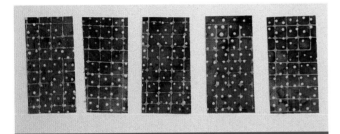

🌸 Leaves and Stems

1. Free-cut 5 rectangles measuring about 1¹/₂″ × 3″ from the leaf fabric.

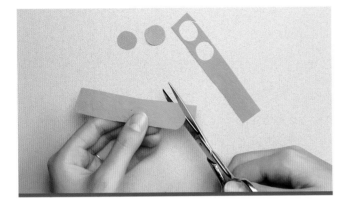

2. Free-cut a short, curved stem about ¹/₂″ long from the center of the 1¹/₂″ side of the rectangle.

3. Free-cut the rest of the rectangle into a leaf shape by moving your scissors in a looping motion around the rectangle.

4. Free-cut the remaining 4 rectangles into leaves.

5. Free-cut 3 skinny rectangles measuring about ¹/₈″ × 6″ from the stem fabric. It may be easier to cut the stems with a rotary cutter rather than scissors.

🌸 Flower Arranging

1. Center the background fabric on the batting and backing fabric. Fuse-tack into place.

2. Arrange and rearrange the flowers, stems, and leaves on the background fabric until you feel at ease with the composition. (Refer to **Shape and Balance** on page 20.)

3. Make sure that there is at least 1″ of space between the flowers and leaves and the edges of the background fabric. The fused binding will overlap the quilt top and will cover any design elements that are too close to the edge.

4. Fuse-tack the flowers, leaves, and stems into place.

❁ Completing the Posy Picture

Refer to pages 60–67 for complete descriptions of finishing techniques.

1. Press the quilt with steam to set the glue.

2. Hand stitch and embroider the quilt with the embroidery thread.

3. Trim the quilt square with a quilting ruler and rotary cutter.

4. Bind the quilt.

5. Add a loop to display the quilt.

POSIES, 7″ × 10¹/₂″, by Louise Wasilowski

Free-cut flowers from pieces of fabric in other geometric shapes such as triangles, rectangles, or ovals.

❁ Variations on a Theme

Congratulations! You have made your first free-cut fused quilt! You are now granted an official Artistic License to Fuse. To keep your license up to date, try these free-cut variations. One hint: the more you practice free-cutting, the more your own style will emerge.

- Small decorative motifs are invaluable design elements. Practice cutting dots, X's, O's, stars, and triangles and save them to decorate a later project. (Refer to the *Tea Time* project on pages 27–33.)

- Free-cut the letters of your name from fused fabric. Remember that some letters, such as the letter "B," are easily reversed. Make sure the glue side is down when you cut out the letter.

- Experiment with free-cutting different edging motifs such as wave, loop, gear, sawtooth, and scallop. Or use decorative blades to cut the fabrics. (Refer to **Cutting with Decorative Blades** on page 14.)

FLOWERS OF THE FIELD I, 24″ × 18″, by Laura Wasilowski

Cut stems and leaves on the bias. Bias-cut fabrics will bend and curve as you fuse them down.

FLOWERS OF THE FIELD II, 18″ × 24″, by Laura Wasilowski

Stack shapes on top of each other to make more complex flowers.

Shape and Balance

A fundamental design element in quiltmaking is **shape**. Shape is the contour, or outline, of a piece of fabric. Unlike many traditional quilts, which are composed of geometric shapes, fused quilts often incorporate irregular and organic shapes. Fusing allows more artistic freedom because there are no limitations on fused fabric shapes.

As in the *Posy Picture* project, free-cutting allows you to make any shape you want. Shapes may be rigid or curvy, large or small. They can be jagged, smooth, geometric, or organic. Free-cut shapes can overlap each other and form new shapes. Using a variety of shapes and sizes in your work brings it to life.

Balance is what gives your quilt a feeling of equilibrium. It's a feeling that all the elements hold together and are placed in a comfortable manner. Arranging the flowers and leaves on the background fabric of your *Posy Picture* is just like arranging the furniture in your living room. Place the flowers and leaves on the background fabric and move them around, trying various positions. They may overlap each other or be at various heights. The arrangement must flow like the space in your living room, neither too close and confining nor too distant and scattered. Rely upon your intuitive sense of balance; it will never fail you.

Country Cottage

AN EASY COLLAGE LANDSCAPE QUILT

Quiltmakers are good at planning quilts. We plan the design and size. We visualize the color placement and fabric textures. We spend hours mulling over the right quilting thread to make the right quilting pattern. Someday we will actually make the quilt!

Fused quilts are fast, but they take a little planning too. Fused quilts are made up of layers of fabric. The first thing you have to plan is the order of assembly of those fused layers. Do you build it from the top layer down or from the bottom layer up?

In *Posy Picture,* you free-cut the flowers and leaves and then placed them on a background fabric. You built the quilt from the top layer down. The size of the flowers and leaves determined how big the background fabric would be and how big the quilt would be.

In *Country Cottage,* you build the quilt from the bottom layer up. The size of the quilt is determined by the size of the background collage. In this case, it's a collage that also forms a landscape with additional layers on top. This second method of assembling a quilt, *fused collage,* is a basic fusing technique. It will be used in future projects as well.

COUNTRY COTTAGE, $9^{1}/_{2}'' \times 12^{1}/_{2}''$, by Laura Wasilowski

MATERIALS

Refer to pages 12–15 for complete descriptions of fusing techniques, including ironing fusible web to fabric, removing release paper, and fuse-tacking.

- **Sky fabric:** 5˝ × 10˝ of a light value color
- **Hill fabric:** 3˝ × 10˝ of a dark value color
- **Field and binding fabric:** 14˝ × 14˝ of a medium value color
- **River fabric:** 4˝ × 12˝ of a medium value color
- **House fabric:** 5˝ × 5˝ of a medium value color
- **Roof fabric:** 5˝ × 5˝ of a dark value color
- **Tree fabric:** 4˝ × 4˝ of a medium value color
- **Shrub fabric:** 4˝ × 4˝ of a medium value color
- **Grass fabric:** 5˝ × 10˝ of a medium value color

- **Flower fabric:** 4˝ × 4˝ of a medium value color
- **Backing fabric:** 11˝ × 13˝
- **Fusible web:** 1¹⁄₂ yards
- **Batting:** 11˝ × 13˝
- **Size 8 or 12 embroidery thread** for quilting (optional)

ADDITIONAL TOOLS

- **Release paper:** 14˝ × 14˝
- **Hand embroidery needle** (optional)

Preparation

1. This quilt measures about 9¹⁄₂˝ × 12¹⁄₂˝ upon completion. It may be hand quilted and embroidered or machine quilted.

2. Assemble all the materials and tools listed.

3. Fuse all the fabrics—except the backing fabric—and remove the release paper.

4. Save the 14˝ × 14˝ piece of release paper from the field and binding fabric for building the collage. This quilt is assembled on that piece of release paper.

Collage Building

1. Free-cut the sky fabric to measure about 4˝ × 10˝.

2. Free-cut the hill fabric to measure about 10˝ wide by 1¹⁄₂˝ to 2˝ high with peaks and valleys. Try cutting with a decorative blade for added interest. (Refer to **Cutting with Decorative Blades** on page 14.) The hills in the sample were cut with a pinking blade.

3. Free-cut the field fabric to measure about 6˝ × 10˝. Save the remaining piece of this fabric for the binding.

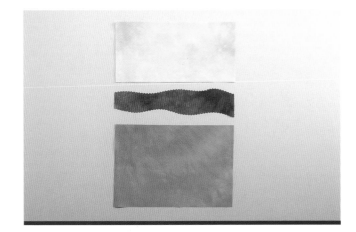

4. Place the sky fabric horizontally across the top of the release paper.

5. Overlap the hill fabric by about ¹⁄₄˝ in the shallowest valley on top of the sky fabric. (Refer to the **Overlap/Under-lap Process** on page 14.)

6. Slip the field fabric under the hill fabric. Under-lap the hill fabric by about ¹⁄₄″ at the shallowest valley.

7. Fuse-tack the sky, hill, and field fabrics together into a collage.

House and Garden

1. Beginning on the 4″ side, free-cut the river fabric rectangle into a tapered, wavy shape that measures about ¹⁄₄″ wide at one end and 3″ wide at the other end. The river will measure from ¹⁄₄″ to 3″ wide by about 12″ long upon completion.

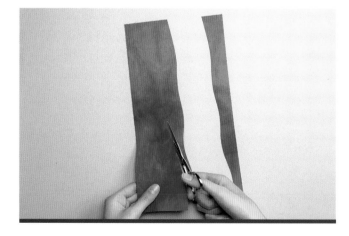

2. Place the ¹⁄₄″-wide end of the river on the upper right of the field fabric, just below the hills. Let it extend ¹⁄₄″ over the side of the collage. Drape the river fabric diagonally across the width of the field to the lower left corner of the collage.

3. Fuse-tack the river into place.

4. Trim the river to fit the collage corner.

5. Free-cut the peaked front view of a house measuring about 1¹⁄₂″ wide by 2¹⁄₂″ high from the house fabric.

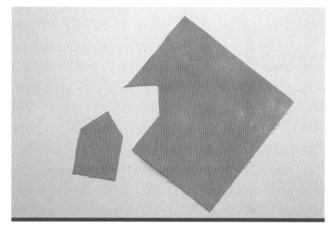

6. Free-cut a strip of fabric to measure about 1¹⁄₂″ × 3″ from the house fabric for the side of the house. Begin at the right bottom corner of the 3″ side and cut at a 60° angle to the top of the fabric. Rotate the fabric 180° and repeat the same cut.

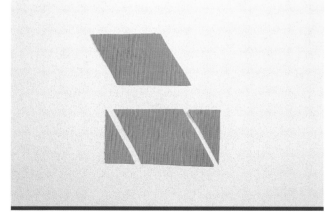

7. Place the house front and side to the left of the river on the collage. Leave a small gap of $^1/_{16}''$ between the house shapes to form a structure line.

8. Fuse-tack the house into place.

9. Free-cut a strip of fabric to measure about $1'' \times 3''$ from the roof fabric. Test the angle of the roof shape by slipping the roof fabric into place on top of the house and trimming to fit.

10. Fuse-tack the roof into place.

11. Free-cut trees, shrubs, grass, and flowers. (The trees in the sample were cut with a pinking blade.) Arrange them on the quilt.

12. Fuse-tack into place.

13. Free-cut smaller details for the house such as doors and windows. Add other free-cut features such as clouds, the sun, or a weather vane to make the house your own.

14. Fuse-tack into place.

Completing the Country Cottage

Refer to pages 60–67 for complete descriptions of finishing techniques.

1. After the fabric cools, carefully peel the quilt top off the release paper.

2. Center the quilt top on the batting and backing fabric.

3. Press the quilt with steam to set the glue.

4. Hand stitch and embroider the quilt or quilt it by machine.

5. Trim the quilt square with a quilting ruler and rotary cutter.

6. Add a loop or a rod pocket to display the quilt.

7. Bind the quilt.

🏠 Variations on a Theme

Use the fused collage as the foundation for both for pictorial quilts and abstract quilts such as *Abstract Shuffle* (pages 42–46). A fused collage quilt can be small like *Country Cottage* or as big as your largest piece of batting. Try these variations in collage construction.

VERTICAL DROP, 17″ × 17″, by Laura Wasilowski

To use the fused collage method for larger quilts, overlap several sheets of release paper to create a piece large enough to build your collage on.

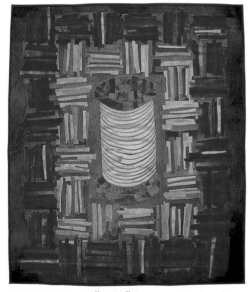

PRETTY SPOOL, 42″ × 50″, by Laura Wasilowski.
Photo by Laura Wasilowski

TOMORROW I, 17″ × 18″, by Laura Wasilowski

Build multiple quilt components on release paper and join them together on top of the batting.

THREE SISTERS, 34″ × 55″, by Laura Wasilowski
Photo by Laura Wasilowski

Change the order of the fusing process: Free-cut elements for the surface of the quilt, then build a fused collage background large enough to accommodate them. This is how my quilt *Three Sisters* was made—the trees first, then the background collage.

Contrast and Value

Contrast in artwork is the interruption of the visual plane. Contrast tells your eye the difference between one shape and the shape next to it. Contrast attracts the eye and can form a focal point or point of visual emphasis like the little house in *Country Cottage*.

The most common way to show contrast is to use different colors for different shapes. You can also create contrast by breaking up a busy pattern with a large unbroken plane, changing the scale of the elements, or placing a recognizable image into an abstract design. The river in *Country Cottage* creates contrast by breaking up a horizontal pattern with a diagonal line.

Another common way to create contrast in artwork is with **value.** Value refers to the relative lightness or darkness of a fabric color. In *Country Cottage,* the roof stands out because there is a change in value between the dark roof and the light sky.

Value can suggest the volume or space of a shape through light and dark areas. It can impart the depth or distance of a shape. Value can also be used to emphasize an element or create a focal point. The changes in value of the fabrics for the sky, hills, and fields in *Country Cottage* define the landscape planes and suggest a feeling of distance.

Tea Time

BUILDING A QUILT FROM FUSED PATTERNS

Walk into any fabric store and you'll be dazzled by yard after yard of patterned fabric. Pattern is the repetition of a motif on the surface of the fabric, or the surface design. There are standard surface designs such as polka dots, checks, and flowers and unusual designs such as turtles on bicycles.

With fusing, you can skip the trip to the fabric store and create your own surface designs at home. Place free-cut dots, squares, or flowers on a solid fabric and quickly decorate its surface. Overlap narrow strips of fabric (*strip-fusing*) and a swatch of striped fabric suddenly appears. You control the colors, the sizes, and the surface patterning of your fabric.

Fusible web also has another unique property that makes life easy. The glue can help you to transfer a drawing of a shape to fused fabric. This quick means of shape transfer is done with a marker and release paper. I call it *shape shifting*. (Please note: The shape shifting method will not work on dark or black fabrics.)

You will use both surface designing and shape shifting in *Tea Time*. The wallpaper

TEA TIME, 18˝ × 22˝, by Laura Wasilowski

and tablecloth surface designs are made with free-cut elements applied to solid fabrics. The striped teapot fabric begins as a strip-fused collage and is then cut out using the shape shifting technique. This is a quick project that will add several skills to your fusing expertise.

MATERIALS

Refer to pages 12–15 for complete descriptions of fusing techniques, including ironing fusible web to fabric, removing release paper, and fuse-tacking.

- **Wallpaper stripe fabric:** 9″ × 9″ of a medium value color
- **Wallpaper fabric:** 9″ × 13″ of a light value color
- **Flower fabric:** 8″ × 8″ of a medium value color
- **Flower center fabric:** 8″ × 8″ of a medium value color
- **Tablecloth fabric:** 8″ × 13″ of a medium value color
- **Teapot fabrics and border decoration fabrics:** 8″ × 8″ of 2 medium value colors and 1 light value color
- **Outline fabric:** 12″ × 12″ of a medium to dark value color to contrast with the wallpaper and tablecloth fabrics

- **Background fabric:** 19″ × 23″
- **Backing fabric:** 19″ × 23″
- **Binding fabric:** 8″ × 26″
- **Fusible web:** 3 yards
- **Batting:** 19″ × 23″
- **Machine quilting thread**

ADDITIONAL TOOLS

- **Release paper:** 17″ × 17″
- **Decorative rotary cutter blades** such as scallop, wave, pinking or deckle (optional)
- **Black ultra-fine-point Sharpie marker or lead pencil**

Preparation

1. This quilt measures about 18″ × 22″ upon completion. It is machine quilted and has a rod pocket for hanging.

2. Assemble all materials and tools listed.

3. Fuse all the fabrics—except the backing fabric—and remove the release paper.

4. Save a large sheet of release paper from the background fabric for collage building.

Wallpaper Fabric

1. Free-cut the wallpaper stripe fabric into 16 long skinny strips measuring about ¼″ × 9″. Use a decorative blade on the rotary cutter. (Refer to **Cutting with Decorative Blades** on page 14.) If you don't have a

decorative blade, use a straight blade and free-cut in a wavy line.

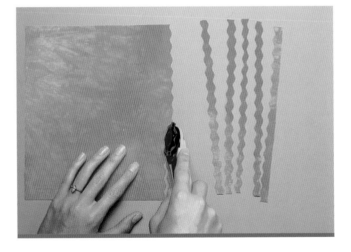

2. Place the wallpaper fabric horizontally on the release paper. Fuse-tack into place.

3. Space wallpaper stripes vertically across the entire width of the wallpaper fabric. Fuse-tack into place.

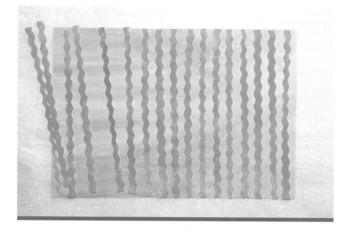

4. After the fabric cools, remove it from the release paper.

5. Trim the edges of the wallpaper fabric by about $1/2''$ with a decorative rotary cutter blade. The rectangle will measure about $8'' \times 12''$.

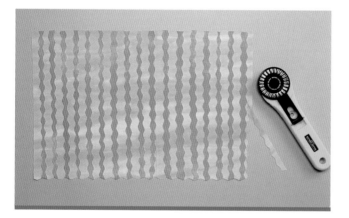

 Tablecloth Fabric

1. Free-cut the flower fabric into 8 strips measuring about $1'' \times 8''$.

2. Set aside 4 of the fabric strips to make the strip-fused teapot.

3. Free-cut the remaining 4 strips into $1'' \times 1''$ squares.

4. Free-cut each of the $1''$ squares into a flower shape.

5. Free-cut the flower center fabric into 11 strips measuring about $3/4'' \times 8''$.

6. Set aside 7 of the flower center fabric strips to make the strip-fused teapot.

7. Free-cut the remaining strips into dots that measure about ½″ across. Cut a dot for each flower.

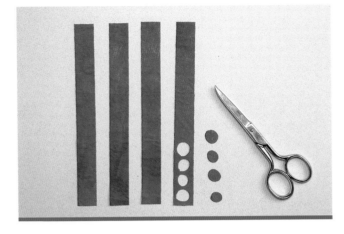

8. Place the tablecloth fabric on the release paper. Fuse-tack into place.

9. Arrange the flowers and flower centers evenly on the tablecloth fabric. Fuse-tack into place.

10. After the fabric cools, remove it from the release paper.

11. Trim the edges of the tablecloth fabric about ½″ with a decorative rotary cutter blade. The tablecloth will measure about 7″ × 12″.

Strip-Fusing

1. Free-cut 7 strips measuring about ½″–1″ wide by 8″ from each of the teapot fabrics. Cut with decorative blades or a straight blade. Save the remaining teapot fabrics for border decoration.

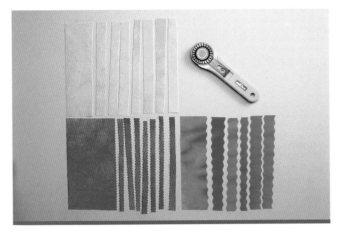

2. Add the reserved flower and flower center strips to the teapot fabric strips.

3. Arrange the fabric strips evenly on the release paper in a striped fashion by alternating colors. Over-lap or under-lap the fabrics by about ¼″. (Refer to the **Overlap/Under-lap Process** on page 14.) Fuse-tack the strips into place.

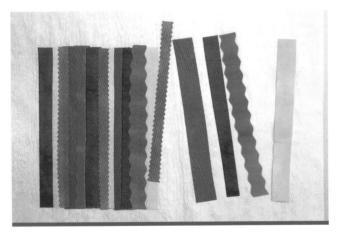

4. After the fabric cools, remove it from the release paper.

✿ Shape Shifting

1. Place a piece of release paper on top of the *Tea Time* pattern (page 36).

2. Trace the outline of the teapot as one unit with a black marker or lead pencil.

3. Move the release paper, leaving about 4˝ of space around the teapot tracing, and trace the teacup, saucer, and a little spot of tea. Leave space around each tracing.

4. Place the strip-fused collage **glue side up** on the ironing surface. Place the ink- or pencil-marked side of the teapot tracing on top of the glue. Position the tracing so that the fabric stripes fall at a diagonal onto the teapot pattern.

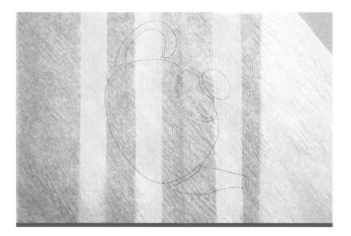

5. Fuse-tack the tracing onto the collage.

6. After the fabric cools, slowly peel the tracing away from the strip-fused collage. The ink or pencil lines will have transferred to the glue. If the lines have not transferred, reapply the tracing and iron again.

7. Roughly cut out the teapot shape from the strip-fused collage.

8. Cut out the teapot parts just inside of the black lines left on the glue. (The black line must be removed or the ink may show through light value fabrics.) After cutting, there will be the teapot body, spout, handle, lid, and knob for the lid.

9. Repeat Steps 4–8 for the teacup and saucer.

10. Repeat Steps 4–8 for the little spot of tea. For the little spot of tea, use leftover teapot fabric rather than the strip-fused collage.

11. Place the teapot parts on the outline fabric. Separate the parts by about ¹/₁₆˝ so there is a small glimpse of the outline fabric around the parts. Fuse-tack the teapot unit into place.

12. Cut out the teapot, leaving about ¹/₈˝ around the edge of the teapot. Do not cut between the joins of the teapot (for example, between the spout and the teapot body). Remove the outline fabric inside the teapot handle.

13. Place the little spot of tea, teacup, and saucer on the outline fabric. Separate the parts by about ¹/₁₆˝. Fuse-tack the unit into place.

14. Cut out the teacup and saucer unit, leaving about ¹/₁₆˝ around the edge. Remove the outline fabric inside the teacup handle.

✿ Tea Party Time

1. Center the background fabric on the batting and backing fabric. Fuse-tack into place.

2. Place the wallpaper fabric horizontally on the background fabric. Center it so there is about a 2¹/₂˝–3˝ border of background fabric showing on the top and both sides. Fuse-tack into place.

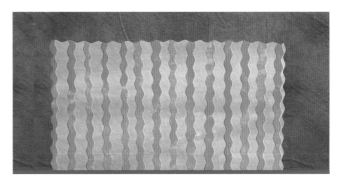

3. Center the tablecloth below the wallpaper and overlap the wallpaper by about ¹/₄˝. Fuse-tack into place.

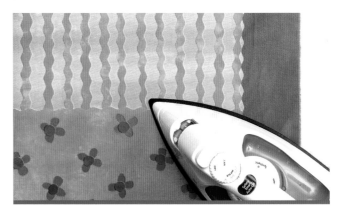

4. Arrange the teapot and the teacup and saucer on top of the wallpaper and tablecloth. Fuse-tack into place.

5. Free-cut 18 squares measuring 1″ × 1″ from the leftover teapot fabrics.

6. Free-cut 18 small squares measuring about ¹⁄₂″ × ¹⁄₂″ from one of the leftover teapot fabrics.

7. Place the 1″ squares around the border of the quilt and add the little squares on top. Fuse-tack into place.

8. Free-cut 6 dots measuring ¹⁄₂″ in diameter from one leftover fabric.

9. Place 3 dots on the teapot and 3 dots on the teacup. Fuse-tack into place.

Completing the Tea Time Project

Refer to pages 60–67 for complete descriptions of finishing techniques.

1. Press the quilt with steam to set the glue.

2. Stitch the quilt sandwich together with machine quilting.

3. Trim the quilt square.

4. Add a rod pocket to display the quilt.

5. Bind the quilt.

✤ Variations on a Theme

To add a little variety to your quilt tops, decorate them with pattern. Pattern is sort of like the icing on a cake. It is decoration both beautiful and good enough to eat. Sprinkle a little pattern on a humdrum fabric and suddenly it comes alive. Explore pattern with these variations:

BIRD HOUSE #8, 14″ × 22″, by Laura Wasilowski

Adapt patterns on everyday objects such as wrapping paper, wallpaper, or even floor tiles, to use as patterns to inspire a quilt.

UNDER AN OLIVE SKY, 30″ × 43″, by Laura Wasilowski
Photo by Laura Wasilowski

Build patterns with stacked components such as dots on dots or squares on squares. Try more complicated patterns that interlock or overlap.

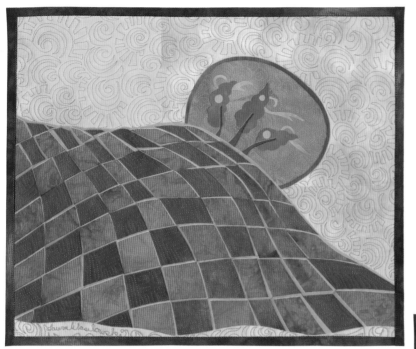

CHECKERBOARD HILL #1, 20″ × 17″, Laura Wasilowski

Use the shape shifting technique to make more complicated patterns. To make the undulating checks as in *Checkerboard Hill,* draw the checkerboard on release paper and transfer the drawing onto 2 fused fabrics (Color A and Color B). Cut out the squares and keep them in order. Alternate squares of Color A with squares of Color B on a background fabric. Alternate the remaining squares on a different background fabric. Fuse and you have two complex checkerboard fabrics made at one time.

CHECKERBOARD HILL #2, 20″ × 17″, Laura Wasilowski

Pattern is the repetition of elements or motifs on a surface. In *Tea Time,* changes in surface pattern delineate the areas of the wallpaper and tablecloth. The striped pattern of the teapot and teacup helps define their shapes so they stand out from other areas of the composition. To break up flat areas and to add interest to your composition, you decorated the border with a pattern of little squares.

Texture is the surface character of a quilt, the raised and lowered areas. Just like in a traditional quilt, the texture in fused art quilts is created through hand or machine quilting. Stitching through the three layers of a quilt creates the relief, or raised and lowered surface, of the piece. It's the textural quality of quilts that makes you yearn to touch them.

Pattern and Texture

Little spot of tea

Lazy Log Cabin

ADAPTING A TRADITIONAL QUILT BLOCK TO A FUSED COMPOSITION

LAZY LOG CABIN, 17″ × 17″, by Laura Wasilowski

The rich history of traditional quilts is a gift to us all. These sewn, or pieced, quilts are composed of blocks, sets of geometric shapes that form a pattern. The number of beautiful quilt blocks to explore is infinite, and they are often the inspiration for modern quiltmakers.

An old standard, the Log Cabin block, can easily be adapted to fusing. Making the fused block is similar to the traditional construction process except for one important factor—there are no sewn seams. For the fused Log Cabin, the overlap replaces the stitched seam. Fusing is a fast and enjoyable way to make this time-honored quilt block.

MATERIALS

Refer to pages 12–15 for complete descriptions of fusing techniques, including ironing fusible web to fabric, removing release paper, and fuse-tacking.

- **Center square fabric:** 8″ × 8″ of a light value color
- **Revolving fabrics:** 8″ × 8″ each of 6 medium value colors
- **Background fabric:** 18″ × 18″
- **Backing fabric:** 18″ × 18″
- **Binding fabric:** 8″ × 22″

- **Fusible web:** 3 yards
- **Batting:** 18″ × 18″
- **Machine quilting thread**

ADDITIONAL TOOLS

- **Release paper:** 17″ × 17″

Preparation

1. This quilt measures about 17″ × 17″ upon completion. It is machine quilted and has a rod pocket for hanging.

2. Assemble all materials and tools listed.

3. Fuse all the fabrics—except the backing fabric—and remove the release paper.

Building Log Cabins

1. Free-cut 1 strip about 1¹/₂″ wide, then cut 4 squares measuring about 1¹/₂″ × 1¹/₂″ from the center square fabric.

2. Free-cut 2 rectangular strips measuring about 1″ × 8″ from each of the 6 revolving fabrics.

3. Free-cut strips measuring about ³/₄″ × 8″ or ¹/₂″ × 8″ from the rest of the revolving fabrics. The Log Cabin design will be more interesting if the revolving fabric strips are not all the same width. To add a little tilt to the cabin, taper the strips from a narrow width at one end to a wider width at the other end.

4. Place a center square fabric in the middle of the release paper. Fuse-tack into place.

5. Place a revolving fabric strip on the left side of the center square fabric to estimate the length of the center fabric, and cut the revolving strip to that length.

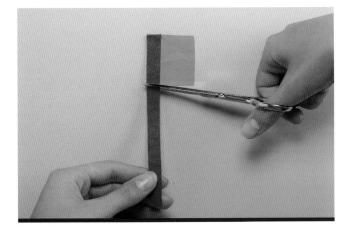

6. Overlap the strip on the center square fabric by about ¹/₄˝. (Refer to the **Overlap/Under-lap Process** on page 14.) Fuse-tack into place.

7. Place a second revolving fabric strip across the top of the 2 joined fabrics to estimate the length of the joined fabrics, and cut the revolving strip to that length.

8. Overlap the second strip on the 2 previously joined fabrics. Fuse-tack into place.

9. Continue to add revolving fabric strips around the collage in a clockwise fashion until the collage measures about 6˝ × 6˝. The collage does not have to be square.

10. After the fabric cools, remove it from the release paper.

11. Make 3 more Log Cabin collages by repeating Steps 4–10.

Framing the Log Cabin

1. Center the background fabric on the batting and backing fabric. Fuse-tack into place.

2. Arrange the 4 Log Cabin collages on the background fabric in a grid pattern. Space the Log Cabins about 1¹/₂˝ to 2˝ in from the edges of the background fabric.

3. When positioning the Log Cabins, be aware of color placement as well as the relationship that each block has to its neighbor. Shift the Log Cabins until they appear balanced and unified.

4. Fuse-tack the Log Cabins into place.

Completing the Lazy Log Cabin

Refer to pages 60–67 for complete descriptions of finishing techniques.

1. Press the quilt with steam to set the glue.

2. Stitch the quilt sandwich together with machine quilting.

3. Trim the quilt square.

4. Add a rod pocket to display the quilt.

5. Bind the quilt.

Variations on a Theme

Traditional quilt blocks provide hundreds of designs that are easily adapted to fused fabrics. I find building a traditional block with fusing techniques to be very liberating because there are no templates to follow, seam allowances to adhere to, or measurements to abide by. Experiment with these variations on the Log Cabin block and set yourself free!

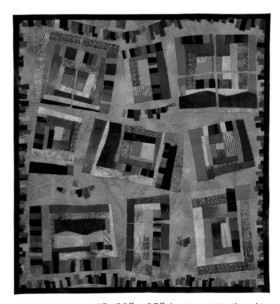

LAZY LOG CABIN #3, 23″ × 25″, by Laura Wasilowski

Make several Log Cabin blocks with different dimensions and combine them.

Cut some of the rotating fabrics with decorative blades. Or add strip-fused rectangles to the rotating fabrics. (Refer to **Strip-Fusing** on page 30.)

RAIL FENCE, 16″ × 21″, by Laura Wasilowski

Select any of hundreds of traditional quilt block patterns and adapt their construction to fusing techniques.

LAZY LOG CABIN #2, 19″ × 23″,
by Laura Wasilowski

Add free-cut elements such as dots
or X's to the surface of the block.

Color, or hue, instantly evokes an emotional response and feeds the eye information about size, shape, and space. It may also give a composition a focal point or be the means to unify it. The *Lazy Log Cabin* is a great opportunity to experiment with color and the placement of color within a composition.

Movement is produced by the placement of shapes and color in the picture plane so that the viewer's eye is directed around the piece. The colorful revolving fabric strips in your *Lazy Log Cabin* are eye-catching, and they are also cut at a slant to add visual interest and excitement.

By repeating lines, shapes, or colors within an art piece, you create ***rhythm***. In *Lazy Log Cabin,* similar components or units (the revolving fabrics) are repeated in a rhythmic manner around the center square fabric. This orderly repetition evokes a feeling of harmony. And, as is common in many traditional quilts, the repetition, or the rhythmic placement, of the individual Log Cabin blocks unifies your quilt design.

Color, Movement, and Rhythm

Abstract Shuffle
A QUICK FREE-FORM QUILT

ABSTRACT SHUFFLE #1, 15″ × 15″, by Laura Wasilowski

Fusing is a quick way to make free-form quilts. Free-form or abstract quilts are invigorating to make and exciting to view, but they have no exact formula for construction. They are based upon improvisation.

Fused improvisation means that there is no preview of the quilt design. The quilt begins as a collage that is cut apart and reassembled any number of times. With each cut, shuffle, and overlap, the quilt is reinvented. You must improvise and make decisions as you go.

The *Abstract Shuffle* quilt is only a taste of the freedom that fused improvisation can grant. It has an easy beginning and a surprising finish.

MATERIALS

Refer to pages 12–15 for complete descriptions of fusing techniques, including ironing fusible web to fabric, removing release paper, and fuse-tacking.

- **Block fabrics:** 12″ × 12″ each of 3 medium value colors
- **Insert and binding fabric:** 18″ × 18″ of a dark value color
- **Border fabric:** 16″ × 16″ of a light or medium value color
- **Backing fabric:** 16″ × 16″

- **Fusible web:** 3 yards
- **Batting:** 16″ × 16″
- **Machine quilting thread**

ADDITIONAL TOOLS

- **Release paper:** 17″ × 17″

A note on selecting fabrics for this project: Keep them simple. Fabrics with a lot of printed surface texture or wild patterns tend to blur the improvisational designs that the shuffling technique generates.

Preparation

1. This quilt measures about 15″ × 15″ upon completion. It is machine quilted and has a rod pocket for hanging.

2. Assemble all the materials and tools listed.

3. Fuse all the fabrics—except the backing fabric—and remove the release paper.

Doing the Shuffle

1. Free-cut 3 squares measuring 3″ × 3″ from the each of the 3 medium value block fabrics. (Refer to the discussion on Free-Cutting in the *Posy Picture* project on page 16.) There will be a total of 9 squares.

2. Free-cut 6 strips measuring about ¹/₂″ × 12″ from the insert fabric. Save the remaining piece of this fabric for the binding.

3. Place 3 rows of 3 squares on the release paper. Alternate the colors so that no two squares of the same color are touching.

4. Overlap and under-lap the squares by about ¹/₄″ to build a collage. (Refer to the **Overlap/Under-lap Process** on page 14.) Fuse-tack into place.

5. After the fabric cools, remove it from the release paper.

6. Free-cut about 1¹/₂˝ from the right side of the collage.

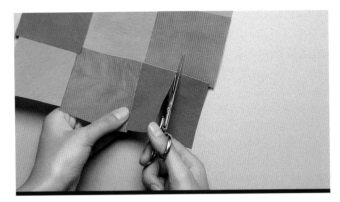

7. Place the 2 collage units on the release paper as if they were still joined. Slip, or shuffle, the right collage down about ¹/₂˝ from the initial alignment. Fuse-tack the 2 collage units to the release paper.

8. Overlap an insert strip on top of the collage so that it covers both edges of the join. Cut the insert to extend about ¹/₂˝ beyond each edge of the collage. Fuse-tack into place.

9. After the fabric cools, remove it from the release paper.

10. Free-cut about 1¹/₂˝ from the left side of the collage, parallel to the first insert fabric.

11. Place the collage units on the release paper and shuffle the left collage up about ³/₄˝ from the initial alignment. Fuse-tack the 2 collages into place.

12. Repeat Steps 8 and 9.

13. Free-cut vertically through the center of the collage.

14. Place the collage units on the release paper and shuffle the right collage up about 1˝ from the initial alignment. Fuse-tack the 2 collages into place.

15. Repeat Steps 8 and 9.

16. Rotate the collage clockwise 90º so the insert fabrics are now horizontal.

17. Repeat Steps 6–15 with this exception: Free-cut 2¹/₂″ from the right and left sides.

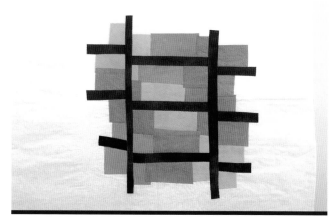

Free-cut the left side, shuffle, and join.

Free-cut the center, shuffle, and join.

Framing the Shuffled Collage

1. Free-cut 4 strips measuring about 4″ × 16″ from the border fabric.

2. Place the shuffled collage in the center of the release paper.

3. Slip a border strip ¹/₄″ under the right side of the shuffled collage. The edge of the collage will overlap the border strip by ¹/₄″–1¹/₂″ in different areas.

4. Center the collage on top of the border strip. The strip will extend about 2¹/₂″ beyond the furthest points of the top and bottom of the collage. Fuse-tack into place.

5. Repeat Steps 3 and 4 on the left side of the shuffled collage.

6. Slip a border strip ¹/₄″ under the top of the shuffled collage and ¹/₄″ under the 2 side border strips. Cut the top strip to length. Fuse-tack into place.

7. Repeat Step 6 on the bottom side of the collage.

8. After the fabric cools, remove it from the release paper.

Completing the Abstract Shuffle Project

Refer to pages 60–67 for complete descriptions of finishing techniques.

1. Center the quilt top on the batting and backing fabric.

2. Press the quilt with steam to set the glue.

3. Stitch the quilt sandwich together with machine quilting.

4. Trim the quilt square.

5. Add a rod pocket to display the quilt.

6. Bind the quilt.

Variations on a Theme

Improvisational fusing has endless variations and serendipitous results. Each quilt is an exciting exploration of unknown territory. If you wish to live dangerously, try these variations on the shuffling process.

COLOR CHIPS AND SALSA #2, 18″ × 18″, by Laura Wasilowski

Build several shuffled collages and combine them into larger pieces.

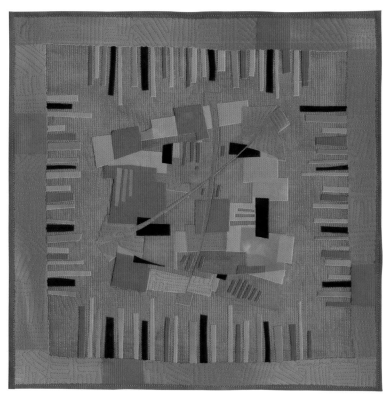

ABSTRACT SHUFFLE #2, 18˝ × 18˝, by Laura Wasilowski

Add elements such as dots, spirals, and squares to the surface of the collage before and after cutting.

Cut the fused collage diagonally or with wavy or curved lines.

SILK SAMPLER VI, 14^1/2˝ × 18˝, by Laura Wasilowski

Overlap free-cut collage units without an insert fabric. Shuffle the units in different rotations.

Proportion is the relationship between design elements based upon their size, quantity, or emphasis. In *Abstract Shuffle,* the sizes and number of elements are quickly changed by cutting. The emphasis on or the importance of an element also shifts as the elements are shuffled.

This fluid building process magically lends itself to another important design principle: *variety.* An array of design elements in different sizes, positions, colors, values, and textures adds excitement to a piece. Improvising with fabric collage, like that in the *Abstract Shuffle,* definitely breaks up the monotony.

Proportion and Variety

Birds of a Feather
A WOODCUT QUILT INSPIRED BY A DESIGN TRIGGER

BIRDS OF A FEATHER, 13″ × 15″, by Laura Wasilowski

On days when my creativity dries up like a lake bed in Nevada, I search for inspiration from a *design trigger*. A design trigger is a fused fabric scrap, or *confetti,* that triggers an image in my mind—like a fish, a cloud, or a bird. Design triggers have initiated some of my favorite quilts and have led to pieces I might never have discovered or imagined otherwise.

Birds of a Feather is based upon the design trigger process and is assembled using a technique I call **woodcut quilts**. In woodcut quilts, fabrics are arranged on a black base fabric that forms outlines similar to those in a woodcut print. Woodcut quilts, with their strong images and well-defined shapes, have a graphic quality I enjoy.

MATERIALS

Refer to pages 12–15 for complete descriptions of fusing techniques, including ironing fusible web to fabric, removing release paper, and fuse-tacking.

- **Black base fabric:** 14″ × 16″

- **Fused confetti,** or **fabric scraps,** from previous projects

- **Bird's head fabric:** 2″ × 3″

- **Bird's breast fabric:** 4″ × 5″

- **Grass fabric:** 3″ × 14″

- **Background fabric:** 14″ × 16″ of a light value color

- **Backing fabric:** 14″ × 16″

- **Binding fabric:** 6″ × 18″

- **Fusible web:** 1½ yard

- **Batting:** 14″ × 16″

- **Machine quilting thread**

ADDITIONAL TOOLS

- **Release paper:** 3″ × 14″ for the grass pattern; 14″ × 16″ for the background pattern

- **Lead pencil or ultra-fine-point Sharpie marker**

Preparation

1. This quilt measures about 13″ × 15″ upon completion. It is machine quilted and has a rod pocket for hanging.

2. Assemble all the materials and tools listed.

3. Fuse all the fabrics—except the backing fabric—and remove the release paper.

Design Trigger

1. Center the black base fabric on the batting and backing fabric. Fuse-tack into place.

2. Look through your confetti, or fused fabric scraps, to find a design trigger. For the purposes of this project, select a fabric scrap measuring about 2″ × 3″ that looks like the wing of a bird. Trim if necessary.

3. Place the wing in the center of the black base fabric. Fuse-tack into place.

4. Free-cut a shape resembling a light bulb measuring about 1½″ × 2″ from the bird's head fabric.

5. Free-cut the narrow end of the bird's head (the neck) into a shallow arc. Use the curve of the wing as a visual guide.

6. Place the neck next to the wing, with a ¹/₁₆″ gap of black fabric showing. Fuse-tack into place.

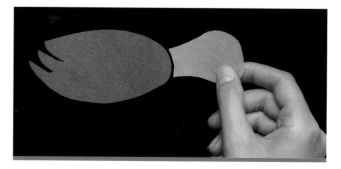

7. Free-cut the bird's breast fabric using the bottom edge of the wing as a visual guide. Cut an arc that slopes around the wing and up to the bird's neck. Test the arc by placing the fabric under the wing. Trim if necessary.

8. Free-cut the bird's breast fabric from the neck area down around the breast to the back of the bird. The shape will resemble a crescent moon.

9. Place the bird's breast under the wing with a $^1/_{16}''$ gap of black showing. Fuse-tack into place.

10. Select 5 fabrics measuring about 1″ × 3″ from the confetti. Free-cut the confetti into tail feather shapes.

11. Place the tail feathers behind the wing where it meets the breast fabric. Leave a $^1/_{16}''$ gap of black fabric showing. Trim if necessary. Fuse-tack into place.

12. Select fabrics for long skinny legs, a beak, crest feathers, and an eye from the confetti.

13. Free-cut 2 long skinny legs with 3 toes on each foot.

14. Free-cut a beak and crest feathers for the bird's head.

15. Free-cut 1 light-colored circle measuring ½˝ across and 1 dark-colored circle measuring ¼˝ across for the eye.

16. Place the legs beneath the bird's breast, and the beak and crest feathers next to the bird's head. Leave a ¹⁄₁₆˝ gap of black fabric showing. Fuse-tack into place.

17. Place the larger eye circle on the bird's head and stack the smaller circle on top. Fuse-tack into place.

 Grass

1. Place the release paper for the grass pattern horizontally on top of the bird's legs at ankle level. Trace around the bird's ankles and feet with a pencil or marker.

2. Transfer the tracing to the long side of the grass fabric. (Refer to **Shape Shifting** on page 31.)

3. Cut out the ankle and feet areas of the grass fabric so the ink line is removed.

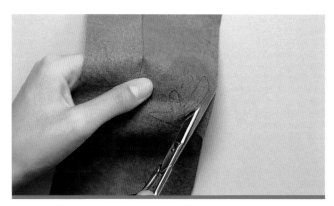

4. Free-cut spiky grass blades around the edge of the grass fabric.

5. Fold the grass fabric and snip out slivers of fabric to form the blades of grass.

6. Place the grass around the bird's feet. Leave a $^{1}/_{16}$″ gap of black showing. Trim if necessary. Fuse-tack into place.

🐰 The Background

1. Center the release paper for the background pattern vertically on top of the bird and grass.

2. Trace around the bird, the grass, and the area between the bird's legs with a pencil or marker.

3. Transfer the tracing to the background fabric using **Shape Shifting**.

4. Cut the transferred shapes from the background fabric.

5. Place the background fabric on the quilt. Leave a $^{1}/_{16}$″ gap of black fabric showing around the bird and grass. Trim if necessary. Fuse-tack into place.

Completing the Birds of a Feather Project

Refer to pages 60–67 for complete descriptions of finishing techniques.

1. Press the quilt with steam to set the glue.

2. Stitch the quilt sandwich together with machine quilting.

3. Trim the quilt square.

4. Add a rod pocket to display the quilt.

5. Bind the quilt.

Variations on a Theme

Be open to the serendipitous nature of making quilts with design triggers. Design triggers free the creative spirit and allow quirky, imaginative compositions to appear that may be quite unlike your regular work.

The woodcut quilt also opens new avenues for quiltmaking. The graphic images made with this technique are dramatic and vivid. Try these different ways of applying your design trigger and woodcut quiltmaking skills.

PHILATELIC FOWL, *32˝ × 38˝,* by Laura Wasilowski

One design trigger may lead to a series of ideas. Make a large quilt with a series of panels based upon a design trigger.

ORANGE HOUSE ON A BLUE ROAD,
16″ × 14″, by Laura Wasilowski

For a variation on a woodcut quilt, use a base fabric of a different color like the yellow in *Orange House on a Blue Road.*

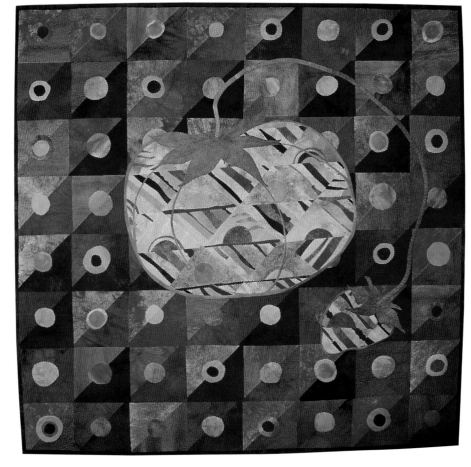

PINCUSHION, 48″ × 48″,
by Laura Wasilowski

Construct a woodcut shape and add it to a collage background.

Line is the outline, or contour, of a shape. In quiltmaking, line is created when two fabrics meet and contrast in color, value, or texture. This contrast is necessary to help define a specific shape. In *Birds of the Feather,* the black base fabric automatically makes the line.

Confetti Collage

A RANDOMLY FUSED COLOR CHIP QUILT

CONFETTI COLLAGE, 12˝ × 12˝, by Laura Wasilowski

Every time I free-cut a piece of fused fabric, I give myself a gift. My gift is the confetti, the piece of fabric I cut away from the fabric. I have bags and bags of these fused chips of color. They are like a stockpile of confetti waiting for a celebration!

Confetti Collage is made up of all the confetti, or cut-aways, you have accumulated from your fusing projects. The fused scraps are instantly ready to make a free, fun collage quilt.

MATERIALS

Refer to pages 12–15 for complete descriptions of fusing techniques, including ironing fusible web to fabric, removing release paper, and fuse-tacking.

- **Confetti, or cut-away fused fabric scraps:** yellow, orange, red, violet, green, and blue
- **Leaf fabric:** 2˝ × 2˝
- **Flower base fabric:** 2˝ × 2˝
- **Flower spiral fabric:** 1½˝ × 1½˝
- **Background fabric:** 13˝ × 13˝ of a light value color

- **Backing fabric:** 13˝ × 13˝
- **Binding fabric:** 6˝ × 14˝
- **Fusible web:** 1 yard
- **Batting:** 13˝ × 13˝
- **Machine quilting thread**

ADDITIONAL TOOLS

- **Release paper:** 17˝ × 17˝

♥ Preparation

1. This quilt measures about 12˝ × 12˝ upon completion. It is machine quilted and has a rod pocket for hanging.

2. Assemble all the materials and tools listed.

3. Fuse all the fabrics—except the fused scraps and backing fabric—and remove the release paper.

♥ Random Fusing

1. Sort the confetti fabrics into 3 sets of colors: a yellow/orange set, a red/violet set, and a green/blue set.

2. Place a yellow confetti piece onto the center of the release paper and overlap with an orange piece of confetti. Fuse-tack into place.

3. Randomly add other pieces of fabric from the yellow/orange set, fuse-tacking them into place, until the collage measures about 4˝ × 4˝. Trim any frayed edges of fabric that may detract from the collage.

4. After the fabric cools, carefully remove it from the release paper.

5. Repeat Steps 2–4 using the red/violet set of confetti.

6. Build a third collage to measure about 4″ × 7″ using the green/blue set of confetti.

Hearts and Flowers

1. Place the yellow/orange confetti collage on the center of the release paper.

2. Place the red/violet collage to the right of the yellow/orange collage. Slightly overlap it on top of the yellow/orange collage. Fuse-tack into place.

3. Center the green/blue collage across the bottom of the two joined collages. Slightly overlap it on top of the two collages. Fuse-tack into place.

4. After the fabric cools, carefully remove it from the release paper.

5. Fold the collage in half with the yellow side facing the red side and with the glue side out.

6. Free-cut the collage into half of a heart shape.

7. Free-cut 2 leaves measuring about ³⁄₄″ × 1″ from the leaf fabric.

8. Free-cut a circle measuring about 1³⁄₄″ in diameter from the flower base fabric. Snip the edges to form a flower.

9. Free-cut a circle measuring about 1½˝ in diameter from the flower spiral fabric.

10. Free-cut in a spiraling fashion into the center of the spiral fabric. The walls of the spiral should be about ½˝ wide.

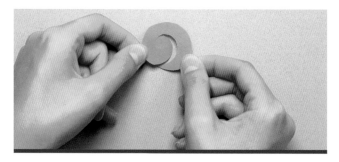

11. Free-cut the spiral wall in half to the center of the spiral and clip to a point.

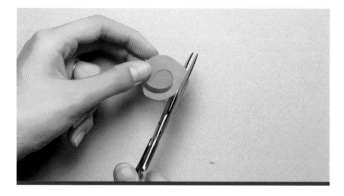

12. Center the background fabric on the batting and backing fabric.

13. Place the heart collage on the background fabric. Add the leaves, flower base, and spiral on top of the heart. Fuse-tack into place.

♥ Completing the Confetti Collage

Refer to pages 60–67 for complete descriptions of finishing techniques.

1. Press the quilt with steam to set the glue.

2. Stitch the quilt sandwich together with machine quilting.

3. Trim the quilt square.

4. Add a rod pocket to display the quilt.

5. Bind the quilt.

♥ Variations on a Theme

Confetti collage is a quick way to tap into an important aspect of art making—play. When you play with the scraps, you intuitively invent new designs. Without realizing it, you are training your eyes and your hands in the skills of making art.

You have now completed your degree in Fusology from the Chicago School of Fusing. Congratulations! In celebration, why not play some more with your confetti scraps? Try these variations on a theme.

OPEN HEARTED, 16″ × 12″, by Laura Wasilowski

Use the negative shape from the heart in the *Confetti Collage* project to make a quilt.

COLOR CHIP COASTLINE, 27″ × 21″, by Laura Wasilowski

Randomly fuse confetti onto a large piece of fabric. Use the collage as a background fabric.

Think of your confetti collage as a sort of journal, a history of all the fabrics you have used in your past fused projects. Make a memory quilt as a memento of your projects.

COLOR CHIPS II,
41″ × 41″, by Laura Wasilowski

Draw a circle or square on release paper and fill it in with confetti fabrics. Add the collage to other collaged shapes to build a larger quilt.

Unity and Emphasis

Unity is the feeling that all of the elements in a design work well together. In *Confetti Collage* you begin with a hodgepodge of fabric and organize it by color to create a feeling of harmony. You can also organize design elements by shape, edge, pattern, texture, value, or line. A unified composition feels safe, like everything is in its proper order.

Emphasis is the focal point, or the place that the viewer's eye is first attracted to in a composition. You naturally seek this focal point; you need a point of emphasis in artwork to give the feeling of harmony. In *Confetti Collage,* the spiral becomes the focal point. This one design element draws the eye and gives you a place to begin the enjoyment of the quilt design.

FUSED FINISHING

You've had hours of fun making a delightful little quilt. Now it's time to finish it up in style. To appear at its best, the quilt must be stitched, trimmed, fixed with a hanging device, and bound. The display and care of your new little quilt are covered at the end of the chapter.

Quilting the Fused Quilt

Quilting is important for a fused quilt. Stitching keeps the layers of a large quilt from sagging and makes the quilt hang flat against the wall. Gravity is kinder to little, lightweight quilts. They don't need to be stitched through all three layers, although quilting does help them hang flat. (Fusing the backing fabric to the batting will also keep a little quilt flat.)

Both hand and machine quilting add a decorative touch to the quilt surface. Quilting patterns or repeated motifs form a relief texture that draws the eye and gives the quilt another dimension. When stitching a fused quilt, you don't need to finish or cover all the fabric edges with stitching. Even the smallest element will remain glued fast to the surface.

HAND QUILTING A FUSED QUILT

You can hand stitch fused quilts with simple running stitches to hold the layers together. Decorative hand embroidery stitches lend a spark of color and tempt the viewer closer. To quilt your quilt by hand, follow these tips:

- Use a fusible web that is easy to stitch through. Some webs are very stiff and may gum up the needle. (Refer to **Fusible Web** on page 7.)

- Use a thimble when sewing. Depending on your hand strength, you can usually stitch through two or three layers of fused fabric. A needle grip may also come in handy.

LOUISE DELAYER, 8˝ × 11˝, by Laura Wasilowski
Hand embroidered with size 8 thread

- Cotton embroidery threads in sizes 8, 12, and 14 are best for hand embroidery of fused quilts. Use crewel or embroidery needles in sizes 3–9.

- Hand stitch the quilt before adding the backing fabric.

- Use simple embroidery stitches such as the running stitch, cross-stitch, seed stitch, stem stitch, and French knot to decorate the quilt. (Refer to **Resources** on page 79 for books on embroidery.)

MACHINE QUILTING A FUSED QUILT

Fused quilts are easy to quilt with a sewing machine. You can stitch up to eight layers of fusing! Both straight stitches and decorative stitches will enhance the quilt. Do overall patterns, stitch around shapes, or fill in select shapes. Free-motion stitching works best to reach those odd shapes found on fused quilts. To quilt your fused quilt by machine, follow these tips:

- Use a fusible web that is easy to stitch through. Some webs are very stiff and may gum up the needle. (Refer to **Fusible Web** on page 7.)

- Use 30- to 50-weight cotton, polyester, or rayon threads in the machine. Match the bobbin thread with a needle thread of the same weight.

Via Pear Mail II, 10˝ × 12˝, by Laura Wasilowski
Free-motion machine stitched with size 12 pearl cotton and 40-weight rayon

- For heavier threads, such as size 12 pearl cotton, use a 14/90 quilting or embroidery needle. Use 30- or 40-weight thread in the bobbin.

- Test your machine's stitch on a quilt sandwich. Adjust the tension of the top and bobbin threads accordingly.

- For additional quilting tips, refer to **Resources** on page 79 for books on machine quilting.

Trimming the Fused Quilt

Before you bind the quilt, the edges must be trimmed square.

Follow these steps:

1. Steam the quilt flat.

2. Place the quilt face side up on the cutting mat. Align the top of the quilt along a vertical grid line.

3. Place the quilting ruler on the top edge of the quilt and align both ends of the ruler with a grid line.

4. Place the rotary cutter next to the ruler and trim the quilt to remove uneven fabric and batting.

Trim the edges of the quilt.

5. Rotate the quilt and trim the remaining sides, using the straight cut edge as a guide.

 Binding the Fused Quilt

There are a variety of ways to finish the outside edges of your quilt. The edge treatment, or binding, finishes the quilt and gives it a proper frame, like a painting on the wall.

FUSED BINDING

1. Trim the quilt square with a ruler and rotary cutter and add a rod pocket if necessary. (Refer to **Displaying a Fused Quilt** on pages 66–67.)

2. Use a rotary cutter with a decorative blade to free-cut 4 strips of binding fabric measuring about $1\frac{1}{4}$″ wide. Cut 2 strips the length of the quilt for the side bindings. Cut 2 strips the width of the quilt plus 2″ for the top and bottom binding.

Cut 4 strips for the binding.

3. Place the quilt right side up on a piece of release paper.

4. Overlap the side binding about $\frac{1}{2}$″ on top of the side of the quilt. Fuse-tack into place.

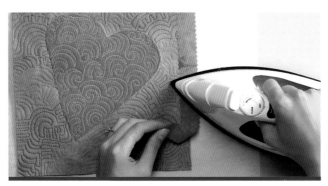

Fuse the binding strip to the side of the quilt.

5. Remove the quilt from the release paper and fold the binding onto the back of the quilt. Fuse-tack into place.

Fold the binding strip to the back.

6. Repeat Steps 3–5 for the other side of the quilt.

7. Place the quilt right side up on the release paper.

8. Center the top binding strip across the top edge of the quilt. (There will be a 1″ flap of binding extending from each end of the quilt.) Overlap the binding about $\frac{1}{2}$″ onto the top edge. Fuse-tack into place.

Extend the top binding off the edge of the quilt.

9. Remove the quilt from the release paper and cut off a $\frac{1}{2}$″ triangle from the corners of the extending binding flaps to remove some of the fabric bulk.

Clip the corner of the binding.

10. Place the quilt back side up on the ironing board and fold the 2 side flaps in toward the quilt. Align the fold with the edge of the quilt. Fuse-tack into place.

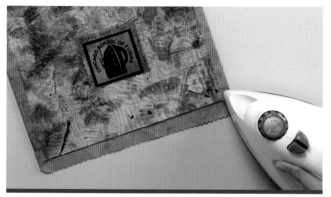

Fold the flap in toward the quilt.

11. Fold the corner of the binding down to the back edge of the quilt at a 45° angle as if wrapping a package.

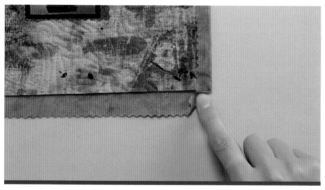

Fold the corner to the edge of the quilt.

12. Fold the rest of the binding down onto the back of the quilt. Make sure the corners are crisp and square. Fuse-tack into place.

Fold the binding strip to the back.

13. Repeat Steps 7–12 for the bottom binding strip.

14. Steam set the binding on the front and back of the quilt.

15. Stitch the binding by hand or by machine.

Stitch the binding.

FUSED BINDING VARIATIONS

COLORADO CANYON, 13$\frac{1}{2}$″ × 15$\frac{1}{2}$″, by Laura Wasilowski

Fuse overlapping rectangles of fabric unevenly around the top edge of the quilt. Fold the rectangles to the back of the quilt and fuse into place.

HOUSE OF CHEESE, 13″ × 15″, by Laura Wasilowski

Use a machine satin stitch around the edge of the quilt.

THREE SISTERS IN THE DESERT, 12″ × 18″, by Laura Wasilowski

Make the binding out of strip-fused fabrics rather than one continuous piece of fabric.

COLOR CHIPS (DETAIL), by Laura Wasilowski

Leave the quilt top edges uneven and extending $\frac{1}{2}$″ beyond the batting and backing fabric. Place a wide strip of fused fabric around the edge of the backing fabric to enclose the batting and to engage the front of the quilt. Fuse into place. Trim the edges of the quilt.

TRAPDOOR OR ENCASEMENT BINDING

Like sewing a pilow, this is a neat way to finish edges.

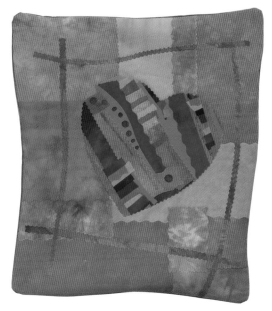

A Joyful Heart #23, 10˝ × 12˝, by Laura Wasilowski

1. Do not apply the backing to the quilt. Hand or machine quilt it now or after Step 7.

2. Stack the quilt layers as you would for quilting and trim. It's okay if the sides wave or curve.

3. Cut a 3˝-wide strip of fusible web measuring the width of the quilt less 2˝. Center the strip 2˝ down from the top of the **wrong side** of the backing fabric. Fuse into place. Remove the release paper.

Fuse a strip of fusible web to the backing.

4. Cut a horizontal slit into the backing fabric through the center of the fusible web, stopping at least 1˝ from each edge. This is the "trapdoor" where the quilt is turned to the right side.

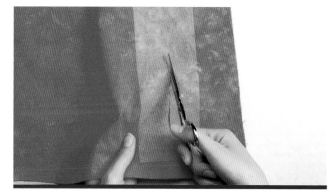

Cut a slit into the backing fabric.

5. Place the **right side** of the backing fabric on top of the **right side** of the quilt. Stitch ¹/₂˝ from the edge around the quilt. Trim the seam to within ¹/₄˝ of the stitching.

Stitch the backing to the front and trim.

6. Open the trapdoor and pull the quilt top right side out, teasing out the corners of the quilt.

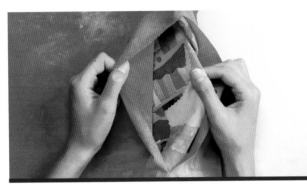

Pull the quilt through the backing slit.

7. Overlap the slit fabrics slightly to seal the back of the quilt closed. Press the quilt flat. Quilt now if you didn't quilt in Step 1.

Overlap the slit and fuse closed.

🔔 Displaying a Fused Quilt

The display method for your quilt depends upon its size and weight. A quilt looks best if it hangs flat on the wall. Choose from these display options:

- Display small quilts, those less than 8″ wide, with a simple loop of thread stitched to the back of the quilt.

- Display the quilt in a shadowbox frame. Stitch the quilt to an acid-free mat. Request a frame that is deep enough so the glass does not touch the surface of the quilt (about 1″ deep).

TINY GARDENS #32, *4″ × 6″,* by Laura Wasilowski

- Drill holes in ¼″ Plexiglas for the quilt corners and a hanging wire. Center the quilt on the Plexiglas and stitch the quilt to the plastic through the holes.

Stitch quilt to plexiglas through drilled holes.

- Display larger, weightier quilts with a rod pocket and a $\frac{1}{2}$"- to 1"-wide wooden or aluminum slat:

1. Cut a strip of fabric measuring 9" wide by the width of the quilt. Hem the short sides of the strip.

2. Fold the strip in half horizontally to form the pocket.

Fold and place rod pocket.

3. Center the raw edge of the pocket across the top back of the quilt and stitch about $\frac{1}{4}$" from the edge.

4. Hand stitch the bottom of the pocket to the quilt back. Leave $\frac{1}{4}$" ease in the pocket for the slat.

Hand stitch pocket to quilt.

- Use Velcro to attach a small quilt to a free-standing plastic photo easel.

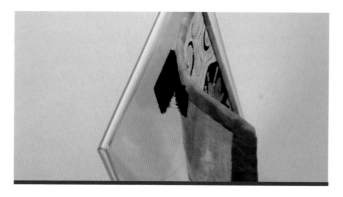

- Add a cuff or strip of fabric to the top edge of the quilt to hook over a plastic photo easel.

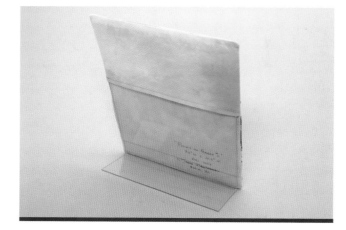

🔖 Care of a Fused Quilt

With proper care, your fused quilt will last a long time. To continue to enjoy your fused quilt, follow these simple guidelines.

- Do not let people handle the quilt. Hands transfer dirt and oil to textiles.

- Do not display quilts (or any art) in direct sunlight. Direct sunlight can damage color and fibers.

- Keep your quilts dry and free of mold and mildew.

- Do not wash a fused quilt in the washing machine. The abrasion of the machine and water may fray the fabrics and lift the edges.

- Clean your fused quilt by shaking out the dust or vacuuming it.

WILD, WILD WEB: OTHER OPTIONS FOR FUSIBLES

Fusers are inventive people. They are constantly discovering new ways to use fusible web and other fusible products to create art. From fusing the hem on a skirt to building a deck of fused playing cards, there is no end to fusing possibilities.

However, there are some things that will not fuse, such as metal and plastic materials. Thick materials prevent the heat of an iron from activating the glue. And materials that cannot withstand the heat of an iron will melt.

COLORADO MARSH, 14″ × 11″, by Laura Wasilowski

PAPER is easy to fuse. Treat paper like a piece of fabric. Cut or rip it to form irregular shapes for collage work, and protect delicate papers with release paper when fusing. If fused papers become warped, flatten them with a stack of books.

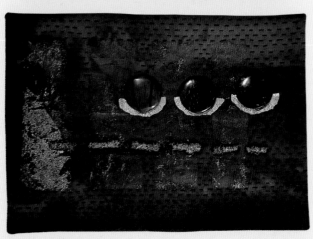

THREE STONES: I, 18″ × 12″, by Lyric Kinnard, Cary, NC.
Photo by Lyric M. Kinnard

Lyric Kinnard has a novel way to use fusible web. She applies metallic paint directly onto the glue while it is still attached to the release paper. After the paint is dry, she irons the painted web to the fabric. The result is a very rich, textural surface, as seen in *Three Stones I.*

INTERSECTIONS #3, 17″ × 16″, by Laura Wasilowski

Fuse **LOOSELY WOVEN FABRICS,** such as gauze or cheesecloth, to add a layer of texture to the surface of your quilt. After it is fused, use a protective sheet of release paper over the open weave to keep the glue from transferring to the iron. Skew the fabric and fold it on top of itself for added interest.

TEMPLE OF THE EMERALD BUDDHA, BANGKOK, 40″ × 57″, by Caryl Hancock, Indianapolis, IN.
Photo by Everett B. Hancock

The reflective quality of **LAMÉ** also adds a glow to a quilt's surface. Caryl Hancock used the sparkle of gold lamé in her beautiful quilt *Temple of the Emerald Buddha, Bangkok.* When fusing the fine lamé fabric, Caryl protects it with a pressing cloth.

SILK SAMPLER IV, 18″ × 20″, by Laura Wasilowski

Fused **SILKS** make beautiful, sumptuous quilts. Treat silk like a regular cotton fabric, but use a protective sheet of fabric or release paper when pressing to avoid iron marks. Sheer silks such as chiffon may show a stain of glue when fused. But regular-weight silks such as China silk, charmeuse, satin, dupioni, and taffeta fuse like a dream. Silks woven with a jacquard print add extra texture to the quilt.

A GARDENER'S PLOT, 40″ × 57″, by Laura Wasilowski
Photo by Laura Wasilowski

A *Gardener's Plot* is made with **CRAFT-FUSE,** a white, nonwoven interfacing with fusible glue attached. To use Craft-Fuse, paint the nonglue side with acrylic paint. After the paint dries, cut the painted Craft-Fuse with scissors, decorative blades, or paper punches. Apply the interfacing directly to batting, fabric, or felt. Cover it with a piece of release paper before fusing it in place.

One advantage the fusible interfacing has over fabric is that it does not fray. But the paint may interfere with the gluing process. Stitching secures the fabric into place.

FUSING IN THE ROUND, 5″ × 4″, by Laura Wasilowski

For my bowl, *Fusing in the Round,* I fused silk confetti fabrics to a long strip of heavy interfacing. The fabric was then folded and hand stitched to a round base.

You now have all the skills a fuser needs. Experiment and discover new ways to expand your fusing knowledge. It's an easy technique with endless possibilities. Press on!

Decorate everyday objects such as playing cards with fused fabrics.

Everyday objects are a great source of imaginative fusing. Apply fused fabrics to postcards and send them through the mail. Make fused greeting cards, journal covers, gift boxes, or even playing cards. Illustrate a cloth book or alter a book with fused paper and fabric inserts.

Inspirational Gallery

AN INSPIRATIONAL GALLERY OF FUSED ART QUILTS

THE CHICAGO SCHOOL OF FUSING, 22″ × 18″, by Laura Wasilowski. *The campus with a view of the Iron Maiden's sports arena.*

The Chicago School of Fusing isn't a real edifice; it's a state of mind. It's a belief that fusing is an easy means to a glorious end, the art quilt. The art quilt is a vital art form enjoyed around the world. And the artists in this gallery have chosen it as their medium.

These professionals produce artwork for sale and exhibit. They teach and lecture about their work and publish books, CDs, and videos about their techniques and designs. Some sell industry-related products such as patterns, tools, dyed fabrics, or threads. Others design fabrics, rugs, and needlepoint canvases. Images of their art appear on prints, posters, calendars, book covers, greeting cards, postcards, and even telephone cards.

I hope you enjoy and are inspired by their beautiful work.

WALKS IN THE WOODS II,
52″ × 53″, by Frieda Anderson, Elgin, IL.
Photo by Frieda L. Anderson

FRIEDA ANDERSON

I choose to fuse because it allows me great freedom in my artwork. The process is fun, liberating, and fast. I have so many ideas, and fusing allows me the speed and the flexibility to make whatever I can imagine. I control the process; it does not control me. I machine quilt my work for the same reason.

ANN FAHL

Fusing is a simple, efficient, effective way to arrange and design my floral quilts. The fused web lends crispness to the fabrics, which adds to the ease of handling. After the design is fused in place, I put each flower in the center of a hoop, and I cover it with free-motion embroidery and decorative thread. I love the texture and dimension this adds to the surface. Fused fabrics do not move or shift in the hoop or under the darning foot, making the task of embroidery easier. When the piece is completed, the crispness disappears, and the fabrics and thread become soft.

AUGUST GARDEN, 48$^1/_2$″ × 48″, by Ann Fahl, Racine, WI.
Photo by Ann Fahl

EMILY PARSON

In my method of working, I use a life-size drawing and a light box, and I pin the fused pieces of fabric onto my design wall. When I am completely happy with the composition, I fuse the fabric pieces together while they are still pinned up on the wall. Fusing enables me to create the large (usually 80″ square or larger) quilts that I envision. There is something very powerful about the ability of large works to physically draw the viewer in, to allow the viewer to experience a work of art to the very edges of his or her vision.

DAFFODILS, 81″ × 81″, by Emily Parson, St. Charles, IL.
Photo by Emily Parson

ROBBI JOY EKLOW

I fuse my quilts because I can get exactly the shapes and lines I want, without having to worry about whether I can turn an edge. *Vessels II* is the second in my fused *Puzzle Series*. I traced the outlines of all the shapes from photographs in magazines, arranged them on the background, and then projected the image onto Pellon fusible paper-backed web. The quilt has a fused binding and was quilted using unmarked free-motion quilting.

VESSELS II: THE PUZZLE, 32″ × 40″, by Robbi Joy Eklow, Grayslake, IL.
Photo by Robbi Joy Eklow

CARYL BRYER FALLERT

I always try to choose the simplest and most direct way to create the images in my quilts. When the pieces are too small or too complex to piece, fusing is the answer. It keeps everything where you want it while you are sewing, and helps seal the edges so they don't fray.

STREAM OF CONSCIOUSNESS #1, 18″ × 18″, by Caryl Bryer Fallert, Oswego, IL.
Photo by Caryl Bryer Fallert

FUGUE VII, 44″ × 64″, by Sue Benner, Dallas, TX.
Photo by John Lanning

SUE BENNER

While making pieced art quilts of dyed and painted cotton in the 1980s, I was also creating original designs on silk. I exhibited these in the form of "paintings on silk," a phrase I used to describe my framed and suspended silk panels. In about 1990, I got up the courage to piece quilts of silk. I loved the resulting works but was frustrated by the process of precisely cutting and sewing the slippery charmeuse, taffeta, and jacquard. A friend and fellow quilter, Gabrielle Swain, told me about fusibles, and I added a few fused squiggles. My next series, *Sink or Swim,* was born from that experimentation. I have been fusing ever since.

SUMMER SURPRISE, $35^1/_2$″ × $35^1/_2$″, by Michele Hardy, Mandeville, LA.
Photo by Michele Hardy

MICHELE HARDY

I love to sew, but I choose to fuse, saving my sewing time for adding lots of thread to complete my images. Spontaneity is an important aspect of my creative process, and fusing allows me the freedom to work quickly and achieve immediate results. My technique involves a combination of surface design, fabric collage, embroidery, and quilting. I construct a background upon which images are arranged and rearranged, layered, machine embroidered, embellished, and quilted. I prefer to have actual layers in my work, which can't be accomplished easily with pieced construction but can be done very effectively with fusing.

MELODY JOHNSON

As a former painter and draftsman, I am concerned with the contours of my shapes, the edges, and I think of them as the drawing line. I like to keep the cut edges of my shapes intact, as they reflect that unique personal touch of the artist. Fusing maintains that edge perfectly. My ideas for quilts are often impossibly complicated, with layers of shapes and colors that would be difficult or impossible to piece or appliqué. Fusing is the perfect construction method for my quilt ideas. I appreciate the immediacy of the technique, which allows me to create on the spot and produce such a quick and clean finish.

TOPIARIES, 52″ × 46″, by Melody Johnson, Cary, IL.
Photo by Melody Johnson

JANE SASSAMAN

My quilts are all appliqué and embroidery. Most of my appliqué shapes are secured around the edges with stitching, and then the background fabric is cut away to reduce bulk and to keep the color as clear as possible. Fusing is used only in special circumstances, either if the shape will be behind all other fabrics (except the background) or if the shape will be a small added detail on top of an appliquéd shape. In both cases, I am adding only one extra layer of fabric, and I am not fusing over seams or multiple layers of fabric. In *Metamorphosis,* the large white butterflies are fused. They are made of a sheer white fabric with white printing. I wanted the blue background to show underneath, so instead of cutting away as usual, fusing was the answer. The stripes on the leaves, the dots on the flower that do not overlap several colors, and the seeds in the seedpod are fused. Generally, I reserve fusing for small decorative details that enhance the larger appliquéd shapes.

METAMORPHOSIS, 29″ × 78″,
by Jane Sassaman, Chicago, IL.
Photo by Brian Blauser

DAVID WALKER

As an artist, I enjoy the freedom of working fast and intuitively. Using fabric lengths that I have randomly pre-fused gives me a creative arsenal to achieve both these goals. Because I enjoy working in a small format, once I lay out the design, press it down, and put the batting and backing in place, I am able to get right to the machine stitching and embellishing. Choosing to fuse has made the creative process more immediate and organic and helps me to sustain clearer and more fluid connections between the idea and the outcome.

BREAKING THROUGH, 12″ × 9″, by David Walker, Cincinnati, OH.
Photo by David Walker

CINDY WALTER

For many years while teaching traditional quilting techniques, I occasionally had an inner desire to make a quilt that was speedy, a project that could keep up with the creative side of my brain. Even strip piecing wasn't fast enough. That is how I eventually invented the snippet technique. To this day my mood still fluctuates. Sometimes I want to sit and hand quilt for hours, meditating on the events of life. At other times I want to "throw" fabric in place and simply create.

I was inspired to make this snippet project because of the excitement friends felt after swimming with dolphins off the coast of the Big Island of Hawaii. The pattern for this project is in *More Snippet Sensations* (Krause Publications).

WILD DOLPHINS II, 36″ × 44″, by Cindy Walter, Honolulu, HI.
Photo courtesy of Krause Publications

About the Author

Laura loves fabric. Her first love was a sweet pink gingham fabric selected for a 4-H sewing project. As a college student, she discovered more exotic fabrics. And while she earned a degree in costume design, she found a new thrill—dyeing.

For many years Laura created hand-dyed fabrics for garments that she sold in boutiques across the country. It was a friendly neighbor who introduced Laura to her current flame, the art quilt. This latest love is a marriage of fabric, color, and whimsy that she truly enjoys.

Laura is married to her colorful husband, Steve. They are the proud parents of Gus and Louise. Laura lives in Elgin, IL, where she hand dyes fabric and thread for her business, Artfabrik.

Photo by David Wilks

RESOURCES

Recommended Reading

All About Quilting from A to Z, from *Quilter's Newsletter Magazine, Quiltmaker,* and C&T Publishing (Published by C&T Publishing, Lafayette, CA)

All About Machine Arts—Decorative Techniques from A to Z, from *Sew News, Creative Machine Embroidery,* and C&T Publishing (Published by C&T Publishing, Lafayette, CA)

Elegant Stitches, by Judith Baker Montano (Published by C&T Publishing, Lafayette, CA)

Snippet Sensations and *More Snippet Sensations,* by Cindy Walter (Published by Krause Publications, Iola, WI, www.krausebooks.com, 800-258-0929)

Threadplay with Libby Lehman, by Libby Lehman (Published by That Patchwork Place, Bothell, WA)

For More Information

Ask for a free catalog:

C&T Publishing, Inc.
P.O. Box 1456
Lafayette, CA 94549
800-284-1114
email: ctinfo@ctpub.com
website: www.ctpub.com

Artfabrik (Hand-dyed fabrics and threads)
324 Vincent Place
Elgin, IL 60123
(847) 931-7684
email: laura@artfabrik.com
website: www.artfabrik.com

Cotton Patch Mail Order (Quilting supplies)
3405 Hall Lane, Dept. CTB
Lafayette, CA 94549
(800) 835-4418
(925) 283-7883
email: quiltusa@yahoo.com
website: www.quiltusa.com

Note: Fabrics used in the quilts shown in this book may not currently be available because fabric manufacturers keep most fabrics in print for only a short time.

Index

🪙 Quilts

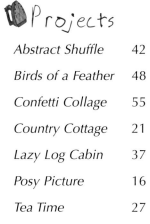 Projects

 Design Lessons